PRAISE FOR
SUCCESSFUL
LARGE
ACCOUNT
MANAGEMENT

"LAMP provides a methodology that enables Price Waterhouse to be viewed by our major accounts as a joint venture partner. It allows us to identify and manage client needs more effectively."
**—Tom Beyer, Vice Chairman,
Management Consulting Services,
Price Waterhouse**

☛   ☛

"We are now in the account knowledge era! The LAMP process helps us recognize it—and that's the start."
**—Brian Cates,
Senior Sales Training Consultant,
Digital Equipment of Canada Ltd.**

☛   ☛

Robert B. Miller rose from associate to vice-president-general manager for North American operations at Kepner-Tregoe, Inc., which markets and conducts seminars and consulting services for senior management of Fortune 500 corporations and for the federal and state governments. He personally sold and consulted with such organizations as Ford, General Motors, Citicorp, and Rolls Royce. In 1974 he founded Robert B. Miller & Associates, where he began developing the sales systems and other programs that were incorporated into operations at Miller Heiman, Inc. He holds undergraduate and graduate degrees from Stanford University. He lives in Santa Fe, New Mexico.

Stephen E. Heiman rose in nineteen years from the level of national account salesman for IBM (where he increased sales in all product areas by more than 35 percent and was in the top 5 percent for total sales and percentage quota) to director of marketing at Kepner-Tregoe, to executive vice-president of North American Van Lines. There he operated as general manager of the $150 million Household Goods Division and with full P & L responsibility, increased sales and profits by 36 percent in four years' time. In 1978 he joined Robert Miller as co-principal and full partner in what became Miller Heiman, Inc. An avid biker and marathon runner, he lives with his wife and youngest son in Reno, Nevada.

Tad Tuleja has over twenty-five books to his credit, including two earlier bestselling books with Miller and Heiman—*Strategic Selling* and *Conceptual Selling*—and *Beyond the Bottom Line*, named by *Library Journal* as one of the best business books of 1985. He lives with his wife and children in Belchertown, Massachusetts.

SUCCESSFUL
LARGE
ACCOUNT
MANAGEMENT

ROBERT B. MILLER AND STEPHEN E. HEIMAN
WITH TAD TULEJA

WARNER BOOKS

A Time Warner Company

Warner Books Edition
Copyright © 1991 by Miller Heiman, Inc.
All rights reserved, including the right to reproduce this book or portions thereof in any form.
This Warner Books edition is published by arrangement with Henry Holt and Company, Inc., 115 West 18th Street, New York, NY 10011

Warner Books, Inc., 1271 Avenue of the Americas, New York, NY 10020
Visit our Web site at http://warnerbooks.com

W A Time Warner Company

Printed in the United States of America

First Warner Books Printing: May, 1992

20   19   18   17   16   15   14   13   12

Library of Congress Cataloging-in-Publication Data

Miller, Robert B. (Robert Bruce), 1931–
    Successful large account management / Robert B. Miller and Stephen
  E. Heiman with Tad Tuleja.—Warner Books ed.
        p.   cm.
    Originally published: New York : H. Holt, © 1991.
    Includes index.
    ISBN 0-446-39356-8
    1. Selling—Key accounts.   2. Market segmentation.   3. Marketing—
  Key accounts.   4. Heiman, Stephen E.   I. Tuleja, Tad, 1944–   II. Title.
HF5438.8.K48M56   1992
658.8′1—dc20   91-41180
                                                                                      CIP

Cover design by Julia Kushnirsky
Cover illustration by Dmitry Kushnirsky

Contents

PART III: SETTING YOUR STRATEGY

PART IV: IMPLEMENTING YOUR ACTION PLAN

PART V: LOOKING BACK—AND AHEAD

Preface

The impetus for this book came one afternoon in Denver while we were conducting a followup program in *Strategic Selling* for the sales managers of a large client company. We were exploring how they might obtain better control in their accounts, particularly their large, complicated, multilocation accounts, when a district manager made a telling observation.

"Your *Strategic Selling* concepts are terrific," he said, "for helping us manage specific pieces of business, like getting a contract renewed or selling something into a new division. But they're not enough. I'm our company's major account manager for Boeing. I need to set strategies to manage the whole thing, not just this or that piece in one division. This is our biggest and most profitable account, but in my opinion we should be getting a much larger share than we are. Do you have any suggestions?"

It was a good question, but it went way beyond what *Strategic Selling* had been designed to do, and we had to admit it took us by surprise. We said we had a few thoughts that might work, and that we'd be happy to share them with him at the end of the day. But the other managers wouldn't let us off that easily. One by one they chimed in, expressing frustrations about their own key accounts. "Jim's not alone," they were saying. "We all have major customers who drive us crazy. How about sharing your ideas with all of us?"

That was the beginning of what became known as the Miller Heiman Large Account Management Process, or LAMP. With what you'd have to call "instant R&D," we ploughed into the managers' shared frustration, and ended up staying over an extra night. By the next morning, we had begun to outline the principles of a novel, indeed radical, approach to large account management.

How radical it was can be understood by considering what the norm was at that time. In those days not so long ago, "state of the art" strategy setting in major companies was what we like to call the Manhattan Telephone Book and Brute Force approach. It worked like this.

First, the company's vice-president in charge of sales sent a letter to all the people involved in handling a given large account, announcing that a three-day "planning session" would be held on October 10th through 12th at the Dayton Airport Holiday Inn. Participants were to arrive the night before, and were to bring with them "all relevant information about the account."

Second, the would-be planners would troop into Dayton lugging voluminous computer print-outs and other reports—any data that might relate, however marginally, to the account. (A sales manager we know who survived one of these "planning" marathons claims that the print-out books for one account, stacked together, made a teetering pile over eight feet high.)

Third, each person at the meeting, flipping through his or her own print-out book, reported to the gathering about "what was happening" in his or her sector of the account. Charts were displayed. Notes were taken. Yawns were heard.

Fourth, after all the individual reports were in, and after the participants had absorbed "all the latest information," a senior manager asked for input from the participants about how the company could improve its share of the account. An endless discussion ensued, with more charts, more notes, and more yawns.

Finally, when everyone was exhausted, the vice-president who had called the meeting announced that he had a plane to catch in forty-five minutes. Turning to the least red-eyed member of the company, he proclaimed, "Doug, you're good with words. Why don't you write up what we've discussed in an account plan and see that everybody here gets a copy."

Doug's resulting "plan" usually came out three or four weeks later. Invariably it included a projection of sales figures based on last year's figures plus an arbitrary percentage increase. It had about as much relation to reality as a campaign promise, and everybody who had been to Dayton knew it. They received their copies, glanced through them at lunch, and put them on their bookshelves until next October, when they would be taken down, dusted off, and dutifully referred to as part of *that* year's "relevant account information."

If we sound cynical, it's not without a good reason. If you've ever wasted three days in one of these make-work, directionless "planning" sessions, you know that we're not exaggerating. You know, too, that you and your fellow account professionals *resent* such charades. You don't have time to spend accumulating huge amounts of historical data, filling reams of computer paper with useless numbers. With all the changes taking place in your accounts and in your own organization every day, the last thing you need is a stack of paper that gives you "instantly obsolete" information.

What you *do* need—what the managers at our Denver meeting told us they needed—is a clearly defined, timely, and most of all dynamic approach to the planning process that can help you manage your key accounts in all their complexity, not just yesterday or today, but into the future. It was to meet that need that we stayed over in Denver after the *Strategic Selling* program had ended, laying the groundwork for what eventually turned into LAMP.

This book addresses, and corrects, the major deficiencies of the three-day yawnfest that often passes for account planning. It is based on over twelve years' experience working with large account managers in client companies like Tandem Computers, Hewlett-Packard, Digital, Price Waterhouse, and AT&T. These and many other clients have participated in the Miller Heiman LAMP workshops. They continue to use the dynamic process we present there to successfully manage and strategize their key accounts.

That process is exactly what is presented here, in the same sequence and with the same direction as it's developed in our corporate workshops. No concepts have been skipped or watered down. You're getting exactly what our valued clients have found useful. In the words of one enthusiastic district manager, the LAMP program is "absolutely in a class by itself—the most valuable account management program in the world today." By the time you finish this book, we believe that you will see what he means.

R.B.M.   S.E.H.
Sante Fe, NM   Reno, NV

Acknowledgments

We would like to express our appreciation to John Brady for his major contributions of concept and methodology that made this book possible. We are also grateful to Diane Sanchez Heiman for her careful editing and skillful coordination of collaborative efforts that went into the completion of the project.

Foreword

At Price Waterhouse, we are focused on client service—and we're using the Large Account Management Process (LAMP) to enhance the level and quality of service we provide to multinational corporations.

Let's start with our firm's mission: to provide clients with value-added services that improve their performance and profitability. This is what client executives expect and demand from us, more than ever before. Here is where the LAMP methodology comes in, because it gives our professionals a framework for carrying out this mission. It's an organized and structured approach by which we can better help our clients achieve their objectives and goals.

The LAMP program is especially useful in working with our many multinational clients. It enables us to be more responsive to the business and management needs of the entire global organization—at the corporate and operating levels, and throughout the various divisions, subsidiaries, and departments.

Using LAMP, our people can gain a fuller understanding of a client's strategic business plan, organizational structure, management practices, information systems, operations, and other critical areas. From this, we can work with management to develop coordinated programs for dealing more effectively with the opportunities and challenges at hand.

As accountants, tax advisers, and management consultants, we're in a unique position to bring a wide range of technical skills and industry experience to each client organization. The LAMP program enables us to identify the biggest profit improvement areas, develop creative solutions, and implement cost-effective plans.

Finally, LAMP gives our people a deeper appreciation of our client's point of view—and how different executives will make decisions in terms of their own responsibilities and priorities. As a result, we're able to work together more closely as a team, and build the long-term relationships that make everyone a winner.

Shaun F. O'Malley, Chairman and
Senior Partner, Price Waterhouse

SUCCESSFUL
LARGE
ACCOUNT
MANAGEMENT

Introduction

"Watch That Basket"

In the autumn of 1909, a Michigan automaker named Henry Ford announced to his startled production force that he was adopting a strategy of extreme specialization. Henceforth his five-year-old company would manufacture only one type of automobile—a "motor car for the great multitude"—that would be inexpensive and invariable in design. Ford called this new wonder the Model T, and quipped that customers could have it in any color—"so long as it was black."

To many people in and out of the automobile business, such concentration seemed crazy. One critic of Ford's single-mindedness is said to have warned him bluntly, "Sounds reckless, Henry, if you ask me. Don't put all of your eggs in one basket."

According to legend, Ford responded with a comment that became a gem of American business history. "Nothing wrong with putting your eggs in one basket," he told the critic tartly. "Just *watch that basket*."

He was as good as his word. Whatever else he may have been, Henry Ford certainly wasn't reckless. As the Model T went into production, he watched his pet project tirelessly. The former mechanic was an early believer in management by walking around, and he did plenty of walking around in his plant, keeping close tabs on that all-important single basket.

The payoff? Six years later two-thirds of the drivers in the country—and one-half of the drivers in the *world*—were proud owners of a Tin Lizzie. By 1927, when the line was finally discontinued, 15 million Model Ts had gone through the Detroit assembly process, and managers as far afield as Paris and Milan were attending lectures on "Mr. Ford's Miracle."

The lessons that would have been drawn in the past from this famous episode would warm the heart of Davy Crockett or John Wayne: "Hang in there," "Stick to your guns," or—in Crockett's own words—"Be sure you're right, then go ahead." They're not bad lessons. But in the reality of today's business climate, they don't go far enough. Good old Yankee "stick-to-itivity" might have ensured market victory eighty years ago; now, as we all tangle with competitors who are even savvier than Ford, and as everyone "sticks to it" sixty hours a week, simple perseverence won't get you a foothold.

But Ford did more than simply persevere. He hung in with a precise, consciously developed strategy of *resource concentration*. That strategy *is* relevant today. In fact, it's more relevant now than it was in Ford's day, because since 1909 businesses have steadily matured, creating far more intense competition in every market and making specialization a condition of survival.

FEWER—BUT BIGGER—FISH

It's no longer enough to gallop out into the marketplace with a dynamite product and a hearty Hi Ho, Silver. Today manufacturers of the best products in the world still have to fight tooth and nail for market niches. Even after those niches are "established," they have to keep fighting to defend them against hungry competitors.

No wonder that businesses large and small are becoming specialized. No wonder that established clothing retailers are moving to designer lines, discrete age segments, and "boutique" merchandising. Or that companies which sold "computers" ten years ago are now focusing on specific college PC markets or small slices of the defense or petroleum industry. They have to—not just to grow but, in many cases, to stay alive. The targeting of more limited but potentially more lucrative markets—of "fewer but bigger fish"—has become an unavoidable fact of business life.

Which is why—today more than ever before—Henry Ford's adage is right on target.

If Ford was around today to translate his observation into contemporary language, it would probably come out something like this:

> If you want to succeed in a competitive environment, you have to concentrate your limited resources on those opportunities with the best chances of high return. Then you have to safeguard your investments by systematically managing those committed resources.

Maybe we're reading a lot into a basket of eggs, but we think this translation, too, is on target. The "systematic management of concentrated resources" isn't a bad thumbnail description of what Ford pulled off with his phenomenally successful Model T.

It's not a bad description of what we do either.

Our company, Miller Heiman, Inc., is a California-based service organization that researches and markets business operations systems for corporate clients worldwide. Our Large Account Management Process (LAMP), one of several programs that we have designed to help managers maintain competitive positions in important accounts, focuses specifically on the most important accounts of all—the customers we call Large Accounts.

Through a detailed and thoroughly field-tested process of Large Account management, we show professionals how to get more for their business efforts by observing precisely the two principles that Ford advocated:

• We show them how to concentrate their limited resources on those Large Accounts where the investment will really pay off.

• Then, to ensure that it *does* pay off, we show them how to manage those committed resources—to protect them against competition and "erosion" as carefully as if they were baskets of eggs.

Obviously, we don't buy the old-fashioned idea that all customers should be treated the same. A nice idea for Utopia, but in the real world the facts are brutally plain: To stay in business today, you have to give not only more attention, but also a more dedicated kind of attention, to "opportunities with the best chances of high return." That's why we focus on the Large Account.

THE LARGE ACCOUNT: A DUAL DEFINITION

What do we mean by "Large"? We'll give you a two-part definition.

The first part is both subjective and pragmatic. "Large" means large in *importance*—importance to you and to your business. Whatever the current figures, whatever the trend, whatever the potential. If *you* consider it important, it's by definition a Large Account.

Think of your critical accounts. The ones that pay the rent and capital expenditures. That account for the bulk of your selling time. And that you're happy to keep knocking yourself out for because you *rely* on them for steady sales income.

Now think of the accounts that have you sweating. The ones with great potential that aren't going anywhere. The ones where you feel under attack. The ones that have you pacing the floor at three o'clock in the morning, with a sales report in one hand and an antacid in the other, worrying about how to keep a major piece of business from slipping slowly, inexorably, through your fingers.

Think, in short, of those accounts that you *cannot afford to do without*. It's those accounts—and accounts with the potential to *become* this important—that we identify as Large Accounts.

The second part of our definition is more objective. It derives from a statistical pattern we first observed a decade ago. We call it the 5 percent pattern.

The 5 Percent Pattern:
*5 percent of your customers bring in
over 50 percent of your business*

When we first identified this pattern in our own account figures, the "weighting" toward those few, big fish seemed excessive. But all of our subsequent research has confirmed the statistic.

Our clients confirm it too. Every sales professional, every marketing manager, every company officer we talk to verifies this pattern. Whether they sell computer chips or potato chips, ad space or hotel space or jet engines, they still take in *half* their total revenues from the same tiny percentage of their customer base.

We do recall one exception. A year ago, during a LAMP program that we delivered to an international division of one of the world's top high-tech companies, an account manager questioned our figure—but only to suggest that it might be conservative!

"It's even worse," he said. "Our revenue figures came out last week. We sell to literally hundreds of customers. This year our *two* biggest clients brought in *68 percent* of our business."

A group of accounts that delivers half or more of your revenues is, by definition, important. So our quantitative part of the definition reinforces the qualitative part. If an account—of whatever "size"—falls into that crucial 5 percent "core," it's clearly one of those "best opportunities" that you cannot afford to let go.

WHAT ABOUT THE OTHER 95 PERCENT?

Whenever we advise a sales team to concentrate on its best opportunities, someone raises this nervous question: "Do you mean that we should be fishing *only* for the twenty-pounders and letting the others get away? Are you advising us to *narrow* our customer base?"

Of course not. Watching the 5 percent "basket" is critical, yes—but it's 50 percent, not 100 percent, of your business. So it's not the only basket you have to watch.

Like most analogies, the one about Henry Ford is not perfect; in terms of current business reality, his quip might be revised, "Put *most* of your eggs in a *few* baskets." We're talking about relative concentration of effort, not tunnel-vision devotion to one client.

In fact, we have found that there are two other categories of accounts that are just as important as the 5 percent "core":

- First, a small group of accounts (usually about 20 percent) that provides an additional 25 percent of sales revenues, beyond the 50 percent we've already mentioned.
- Second, a further set of prospects and small accounts that have the potential (either immediate or long term) to become part of this 20 percent—or even part of the "core" 5 percent.

Far from advising you to focus only on the biggest fish in the pool, we say you should concentrate your resources on *all three* of these account categories. Because they're all potentially, if not immediately, important to your bottom line, we refer to customers in all three of these groups as Large Accounts.

WHAT IF YOU'RE NOT IBM?

Since most of our clients are large national and multinational corporations, we are often asked by people in smaller businesses whether the LAMP program would also work for them.

The answer is an emphatic yes.

In fact, for the person who sells for a small firm, or who runs his or her own small business, the concept of the Large Account may be *more* crucial than it is for our Fortune 500 clients. Because small businesses have fewer customers than large businesses, each individual customer becomes that much more crucial to the business's stability; the loss of a single important account becomes that much more devastating; and the skills of Large Account management become all the more essential to survival.

We have a friend in New York, for example, who runs a small word processing business. His annual revenues probably amount to what General Motors makes in two seconds. But his client list displays the same 5 percent pattern that we have observed in the giants. *One* client, in fact—a cosmetics firm that hires him to format internal documents—accounts for about a fifth of his income.

He takes that account very seriously. When he discovered, about a year ago, that the firm was beginning to consider other vendors, he put all his other work on hold for two days, called on the customer personally, identified the reasons for their dissatisfaction with his service, and fixed the problem. He was able to keep this crucial piece of his business by acknowledging, and acting on, its importance—in other words, by treating it as a Large Account.

The best working definition we've ever heard of a Large Account came from one of our corporate clients. He's a Fortune 500 manager, but his definition didn't mention size. "If it would *hurt like hell to lose it,*" he said, "it's by definition a Large Account."

LARGE ACCOUNTS: YOUR "EXTERNAL ASSETS"

Because Large Accounts are so critical to the survival of modern businesses, we don't consider them simply "customers" or "accounts." We call them *external assets.*

Traditionally, assets are defined pretty narrowly, as the tangible property a company controls. Recently, it's become fashionable to adopt a slightly broader definition. The more imaginative managers today acknowledge that such intangibles as employee goodwill and market reputation might also be defined as assets.

We go one step beyond that: beyond the walls of the company itself into the external world where the company does business. We say that Large Accounts—even though they're "external"— are every bit as important to a company's success as state-of-the-art machinery or productive workers. So they too have to be defined as assets.

And—here's the revolutionary point—if they're assets, *they have to be managed like assets.*

Revolutionary, but also common sense. If you invest financial assets in a mutual fund, you hire a portfolio expert to ensure their growth. If you track shipments and receivables by computer, a systems manager keeps the software up to date. The same degree of attention to safeguarding basic resources—to watching your important "baskets"—*must* apply to every Large Account.

This doesn't happen very often. When we ask our corporate clients how their Large Accounts got to be large, a common response is "We don't know." In some cases, good old-fashioned salesmanship at a few decentralized buying locations gradually coalesced into a Large Account. In other cases, luck played a part: The selling organization happened to be in the right place at the right time with the right product or service to answer an exceptional customer demand. In still others, the Large Account started small and just grew.

In many cases this came about without the selling organization knowing about it until it was an established fact. "You wake up one morning," says one general manager, "and you realize that the Boston group is 8 percent of your business. And you mutter to yourself, 'How'd *that* happen?' "

But—and it's a 24-karat *but*—this scenario is on the way out. The days of Large Accounts that just grew are not only numbered; they're gone.

So are the days when a company could keep a Large Account on the basis of traditional business ties or customer loyalty. It's sad but true: Customer loyalty is almost as dated as the Model T, and businesses that think they can keep major accounts alive without aggressive, studious *management* are falling by the wayside every day.

In today's climate, two facts are plain:

1. The systematic management of Large Accounts is becoming *more*, not less, critical to business survival.
2. Virtually no one knows how to manage Large Accounts effectively, as the major business assets that they are.

In fact, it's not going too far to say that one of the most glaring needs in business today is for a systematic approach to the Large Account that will ensure not only continuity of revenue today, but steady growth of these critical assets into the future. Miller Heiman's Large Account Management Process fills that need.

If you recognize the 5 percent pattern we've identified; if you have a gnawing suspicion that some of your major business opportunities are stagnating or "underdeveloped"; if you sometimes find that your selling energies are being spread impossibly thin; most of all, if you feel the need for clearer *understanding* and better *control* in those accounts that are keeping you in business—then LAMP is designed for you. Your business needs. Your revenue and expense picture. Your bottom line.

PART 1

LAMP's Basic Principles

1

Account Management: Beyond the "Muddling Through" Approach

A couple of years ago, we were seated around a client's conference table conducting an executive briefing for senior management. We had just run a series of programs for this company's major account managers. Because long-range commitment to our clients is a watchword at Miller Heiman, we had requested the briefing for two reasons: to get their feedback on our programs and to explain to their senior management where we felt they were vulnerable to the competition.

We were puzzled about how their company's single largest account was being managed. It was in the hands of a manager we'll call George, who seemed to have every shred of data relating to it locked up inside his head. Judging from sales figures, he was very capable. But the fact that nobody *but* George knew crucial aspects of what was happening in the account made us uneasy. It suggested that the management wasn't managing; they couldn't possibly have a handle on even short-term objectives in the account—not to mention long-term goals—if George was treating this piece of business like his private turf.

Obviously the senior managers were uneasy too. No sooner had we made the observation than the conference table became deathly quiet. Then throats cleared. Chairs shifted. Pencils tapped.

After about a minute of general embarrassment, one of us broke the silence. "I don't know what we said, but I feel like we just laughed at a wake. What's going on?"

The senior manager present, an executive vice president, gave us a straight answer. "You didn't say anything you shouldn't have. In fact, you've done exactly what I hoped you would do. You've forced us to look in the mirror, and I guess we don't like what we see.

"George is the highest-paid guy on the sales force. But everybody here at one point or another has felt he's holding us hostage with that account. We did $45 million with them last year—13 percent of our sales—and yet the account seems to be stagnating. Given the match between our services and their needs, revenues are nowhere near what they *could* be. And none of us really knows why."

With this comment, the floodgates flew open. There were six other executives at the briefing, and every one had strong opinions about George's account.

"George has retired on the job," snapped one operations vice president.

"Retired, hell!" responded another executive. "He pulls down six figures a year, and we consider him a problem?"

"Sure he's good, but he's too much off on his own. We're trusting him to sell *our* services with no questions asked about how. It leaves too much up to chance."

"That's true," the executive vice president agreed. "We see George as a kind of loose cannon. I can't tell you how many nights I wake up at three A.M., sweating about our vulnerability there. The bottom line, I'm afraid, is that we just don't understand what's going on."

This doleful admission proved to be painfully accurate. The company soon found out just how painful.

Among the many things the managers "just didn't understand" was how *George* felt about the situation. If they had talked to him instead of guessing, they would have discovered that he was uneasy too. In fact, he was a lot more than uneasy; he was isolated, irritated, and so uncomfortable that he had begun to consider offers from other firms. About four weeks after that meeting, he accepted one.

By that point he had been "out of the loop" for so long that nobody could talk him into staying, and so management found itself in the infuriating—and painful—position of grumbling as he sashayed out the door.

And the major account he'd been handling?

Well, because decision makers in the customer's organization knew nobody in our client's organization but George, they had felt as isolated as he did. Rather than suffer a potentially disruptive period of transition with an unknown new manager, they opted to follow him to his new company. And our client was smacked with the realization that stagnation was the least of its worries. Almost overnight the problem shifted from a vague uncertainty about what was going on to the certain desperation of a man who was drowning—in $45 million of lost revenue.

WHAT WENT WRONG? THE OBVIOUS—AND THE NOT-SO-OBVIOUS—ANSWER

Every company has salespeople like George: excellent account managers who become isolated in their own companies and end up going over the side. How can this common problem be prevented? How can a company keep its often brilliant, often testy, revenue leaders from becoming, in the executive vice president's term, "loose cannons"?

Today's "people-centered" management theorists would have an obvious answer: There should have been better communication between Loose Cannon George and the company "bridge." If he had felt involved, he wouldn't have left.

True. But that obvious answer wasn't the whole story. When our client asked for our assessment of the episode, we said that the problem cut deeper than lack of communication. It was that senior management—delighted with George's $45 million yearly haul—didn't even *realize* it had a disaster brewing until its isolated star had defected. As long as he kept raking in the revenues, no one ever thought to look beyond the current quarter, to see how this Large Account was being managed, or mismanaged, for the future.

Why? Why would a group of competent managers blind themselves to potential danger? They certainly sensed that something was wrong—all their comments in the executive briefing indicated as much. Why didn't they find out what it was?

"Communication breakdown" is a description, not an explanation, of the problem. The reason that communications broke down—indeed, the reason they were doomed to break down—is that this company, like many otherwise well-managed companies, lacked a consistent *methodology*, or *process*, for handling Large Account information. The company needed a systematic approach to those accounts that went way beyond spot-checking of obvious problems, and that included sales *and* general management in long-term planning.

Because it lacked such a process, the company was bound to run into trouble. It wasn't that the disgruntled executives in the briefing room were consciously excluding George from their Large Account strategy—any more than he was consciously excluding them. *No one had a strategy to begin with.* And there was no format for including everyone in devising one. Our original suspicion had been correct: No one was really *managing* this account. Instead, as the British would put it, they were "muddling through" day after day—until they found themselves *in* a muddle.

FURTHER ADVENTURES IN SNAFU

The Loose Cannon scenario we've been discussing is only one of the varieties of SNAFU that can happen when you lack a consistent process for managing account information. There are many others.

Take, for example, the Kermit Syndrome. We got that name from a regional manager who uses it to describe his own "chronic reactivity." "Sometimes I feel like Kermit the Frog," he jokes. "The customer says 'Jump' and all I can say is 'How high?' "

What he's complaining about here—and rightly so—is the professional seller's tendency to play good provider whether or not it serves his or her own interests—or the *real* interests of the customer. In a common version of the Kermit Syndrome, the salesperson gets an irate call from a customer who wants to know when he's getting the spare part that he ordered two weeks ago. Dropping everything, the salesperson runs to the service department, yells at them in turn, and promises to deliver the part personally that afternoon.

This kind of knee-jerk compliance may look "customer-oriented" on the surface, but it's often a side effect of having mismanaged the sale in the first place. Having given the customer (and the service department) incomplete or erroneous information, the salesperson is forced into a merely reactive mode, and ends up dancing to whatever tune the customer calls. Without a consistent methodology for assessing account information, such mininightmares are inevitable.

Or take the Squeaky Wheel Syndrome—in a sense, the opposite of the Kermit Syndrome. The Kermit company will do anything to avoid trouble. In the Squeaky Wheel scenario, you do nothing unless the customer screams in your face: It's the squeaky wheel—and only the squeaky wheel—that gets oiled.

We witnessed this scenario in operation a couple of years ago, when a consumer products company lost its principal retail client to the competition after what it supposed was a trouble-free "honeymoon" period. Throughout that period, the retailer was becoming increasingly irritated at what it saw as rigid billing procedures. But the consumer products firm never knew about this irritation because it had no way to assess customers' perceptions. By the time management heard the grumbling, it was too late.

Again, a companywide system of managing account information could have picked up on the problem and headed it off. The consumer products firm's If-it-ain't-broke-don't-fix-it attitude simply handed this Large Account to the competition.

THE PROBLEM BEHIND THE PROBLEM: WHO'S HANDLING THE WHEEL?

The three cases we've mentioned here—the Loose Cannon, Kermit, and Squeaky Wheel syndromes—are different from one another in several respects. But the fundamental problem in each case—the "problem behind the problem" in most cases of Large Account erosion—can be stated simply. At every level of the selling organization, the people supposedly in charge of the account *aren't*. Having no established system for managing account information, they muddle, ticking off monthly quotas and hoping for the best, while their accounts drift out of control.

This seat-of-the-pants approach to account management is extremely common in modern businesses. For an idea of how effective it is, listen to some definitions of the word "muddle." Associating it with the noun "mud," our *Oxford Dictionary* gives us the following: "to mismanage"; "to render unintelligible by lack of method"; "to busy oneself aimlessly." Most pointed of all for our purposes: "to waste time or money without clearly knowing how."

The best account managers never "muddle." They are successful precisely because of their method and because they always know the "aims" of their management. In nautical terms, they keep their hands on the helm. Like a ship captain who must constantly check and adjust the course in shifting seas, they keep in touch, on a regular basis, with account activity, so that "minor" problems never get a chance to grow into major ones. They keep on top of changing data because they know they *have* to.

When we make this point in our Large Account Management Process workshops, occasionally someone objects that certain accounts don't really need constant management. They're so solid that they "almost take care of themselves."

There's a world of lost revenues in that "almost." As we point out to our clients, the nautical analogy would be to say that the sea ahead is so placid that you can flip on the automatic pilot and go to sleep. As the fate of the *Exxon Valdez* made clear, when you're responsible for a craft on the high seas, that attitude can be reckless to the point of tragedy. It can also lead to shipwreck in business.

The reason has as much to do with psychology as it does with today's "rough sea" markets.

When a company thinks a Large Account doesn't need management, the assumption is that it's already under control—in other words, that it's a "sure thing." The attitude implicit in such a claim is the most dangerous one any supplier can ever have. Time and again we have seen it illustrate the biblical adage about pride going before a fall.

The problem is not just "bad attitude." It's that, from the

customer's point of view, such confidence always translates into cockiness. If I think good old Jim's account does not require my attention, I will inevitably project that feeling to him. And once Jim realizes that I don't think I have to work for his business, he will start looking for other suppliers. In today's competitive environment, they won't be hard to find.

We make this point in our LAMP programs by asking the participants a loaded question: "How would you feel if, as a customer, you knew a supplier considered *your* business a sure thing?" In a recent program, a regional manager for a large telecommunications firm gave a pungent and perceptive answer: "I'd exchange jobs."

Since exchanging jobs with your sure-thing customers is probably not a realistic option, our advice is to take nothing and no one for granted. If Jim's account is important to your business, give it the attention it deserves.

GETTING BEYOND "YESTERDAY'S NEWS"

By "attention" we mean attention to the *present*. We stress this because most managers don't. With all the goodwill in the world, they try to understand what's happening in their Large Accounts, but they fail because they're looking *backward* rather than ahead.

Take the typical "account plan." It's generally an accumulation of data, including such supposedly useful pieces of information as sample proposals and the latest sales figures. The data are meant to provide the selling organization with an overview of what's happening in the account, but all too often they don't. Why? Because the information is yesterday's news.

We've all seen those twenty-pound account plans that, on close inspection, turn out to be reviews rather than previews of what's happening. That's typical of account plans. Almost by definition they compile "instantly obsolete" information: last year's revenues and brilliant coups and grand mistakes. Trying to bring control into a Large Account by relying on such dated information is like trying to find out where you're going by peering intently into your car's rearview mirror.

Even in those situations where an account plan does address

the future—by projecting revenues for the next accounting period—the forecasts tend to be mere extrapolations of what has happened in the past: "We sold them 500 cartons last year; let's go for 550 this year."

Such projections from outmoded figures are, not surprisingly, seldom accurate. Because they don't take into consideration today's and tomorrow's dynamic realities—including your customers' changing needs—they cannot help you manage your Large Accounts in an atmosphere of constant change.

The only thing that can help you do that is a methodology that is itself dynamic. Because LAMP delivers precisely that kind of methodology, it's 180 degrees removed from the traditional, rearview-mirror way of looking at accounts.

Where others sift through haystacks of static data, searching for elusive needles of success, we apply a unique *process* of information analysis, designed for infinite flexibility in the roughest seas. And where others take the past as the guide to the present, we take the present—in all its challenging mutability—as the starting line for managing *tomorrow's* business. With LAMP analysis, you'll never again have to "muddle through."

Big-Picture Strategy:
The Art of Positioning

"Strategy." It may be the most overused business term of the past decade.

Check any bookstore. The business section will have at least one book on hand at all times with the word "strategy" in the title, while articles promising "Strategies for the Nineties" will grace the covers of several magazines. Turn on the TV. You'll see a different Wall Street whiz kid every week spelling out portfolio strategies for Louis Rukeyser. Take a masochistic dip into the management journals. You'll find such indigestible morsels as "The Suppression of Technology as a Strategy for Controlling Resource Dependence" and "Corporate Strategy: A Cybernetic Perspective." "Strategy" is now used to refer to everything from Japan's national industrial policy to K mart's entry into designer clothing.

When a term becomes as commonplace as this one has, no two people use it alike. Like other corporate buzzwords—remember "management by objectives" or "Theory Z"?—the term "strategy" has been spread so thin that it's become a conversational quark, too speedy to pin down or to understand.

Not at Miller Heiman. We use "strategy" with the same degree of precision that we bring to our understanding of "account" and "management." We have to. In our systematic approach to selling, "strategy" isn't faddish jargon. It's a uniquely defined, central principle of Large Account Management.

A UNIQUE DEFINITION:
STRATEGY AS "POSITIONING"

We first went "public" with our definition of strategy six years ago, in our book *Strategic Selling*. There we pointed out that the word derived from the Greek *strategos*, for "general," and we explained that the general's basic responsibility was to *position* troops effectively before a battle: "Strategy" meant arranging things on the field to your best advantage, so you got the most out of each tactical encounter. It was the same in selling, we wrote. Good sales strategy meant fully understanding your own and your customer's position *before* every individual sales call, so that when that call began, you knew—just like a good general knew—that you were in the *right* place with the *right* people at the *right* time.

In the LAMP program, we focus not on the individual sales call, or on individual sales objectives, but on opportunities in the whole *account* over time. But even though this means the scope of Large Account strategy has to be much wider than that of sales-call strategy, our basic definition of the term is still valid. Good account strategy, just like good sales-call strategy, still means positioning yourself to your best advantage. It still means taking control of the situation by practicing a general-like art of arrangement.

Don't be misled by the military analogy. There are similarities between generalship and account management, but there are also major differences, and this means it's worth repeating a proviso that we spelled out in *Strategic Selling*.

When we use the military metaphor, we're not talking about "beating the buyer." To us, no customer is an "enemy" or a "mark" to be tricked into buying. That old snake-oil attitude toward selling is about as relevant today as snake oil itself. We use the military analogy because it's familiar (whether you're in the "war room" or "out in the trenches") and because it reminds us that in business, as in war, you can get hurt, and hurt badly, if you're "outgeneraled" by the competition. It's no accident that

Business Week speaks of "cola wars," or that sales reps talk of "fighting" for territory. That's the way it feels when you're out there.

We use the metaphor for another reason too. In military terms, it's the general who keeps the big picture in mind. The private in the foxhole, the platoon leader—they focus, typically, on what's staring them in the face. This battle, this hill, this round of shells. The general has to think in terms of *scale*.

A "STRATEGY OF SCALE"

Let's drop the military metaphor for a moment and consider an old French anecdote. It's the thirteenth century, and three masons are hard at work, mixing mortar in a huge cauldron. A passerby asks them what they're doing.

The first goes on stirring. "Mixing mortar," he says.

The second one looks at the sidewalk superintendent for a moment, then resumes his work. "We're filling the cracks in this wall," he says.

The third mason looks up and then gestures, proudly, over his shoulder. Hundred-foot scaffolding embraces a wall laced with ribbons of stained glass. The worker smiles and says, "We're building a cathedral."

There's a very real and pragmatic similarity between the attitude of the one mason who understood he was building a cathedral and the attitude of the effective account manager. The Willy Lomans of the world mix mortar. Most businesspeople are busy patching walls. A rare few see the "cathedrals" in their accounts. Yet those rare few are invariably their industry's stars.

It's not easy to visualize your work on this scale. Seeing the potential cathedrals (or Sears Towers, if you prefer) in your Large Accounts means asking questions that are revolutionary in their perspective. Not just "How do we rope in this piece of business?" but "How does this piece of business relate to other pieces of business that we might realize from this account?" Not "How can we write this order?" but "What *other* orders do we want?" And, even more important, "What orders do we *not* want?"

Most important of all, it means asking "How do we want to be *positioned* with this account after this particular deal is won or lost?" In other words, what are our long-term goals and objectives with regard to this Large Account? And how can we develop a relationship with this customer that will be as solid five years from now as it is today?

PLAYING FOR KEEPS: BEYOND THE QUICK FIX

We live in the age of the microwave oven and fiber optics, the leveraged buyout and instant lottery winners, the Vegas marriage and the Reno divorce. In this heaven of quick fixes, the idea of playing for keeps—of nurturing a dynamic and sometimes difficult relationship over time—can seem as quaint in business as it does in marriage. For many of us, to quote the movie *Postcards from the Edge*, "Instant gratification isn't fast enough."

For this reason, selling people on the value of long-term positioning is seldom easy. Thinking long term is unpopular. In many cases, we'll admit, it's hardly painless. But does it pay off?

It did for a New York insurance carrier that discovered, in the mid-1970s, that its biggest client, a giant textile firm, was entering Chapter 11. Rather than leave this old and valued customer to the wolves—as conventional wisdom might have dictated—the insurance company continued to carry its policies until it reorganized, came back stronger than it had been before—and signed on for vastly increased coverage.

It paid off for a national retailing firm that once unwittingly sold potentially hazardous radios. When two or three of the defective products caught fire in consumers' homes, the retailer made a long-view decision. Rather than relying on its liability coverage to meet the few claims it knew might come in, it discontinued the item and offered every purchaser of the product a full refund. It was an expensive decision, but it secured the retailers' major strategic asset—its customers' trust.

The long view pays off in Peoria too. This Illinois town is the home of Caterpillar Tractor, which in the 1980s gambled millions in sales revenues to test the wisdom of a playing-for-keeps time frame. After the 1982 recession gutted the heavy construction markets, Cat endured crippling strikes, saw its market share drop eleven points, and was hit by competition from Japan's Komatsu company that undersold its products by 40 percent. Among the measures Cat employed to slow the hemorrhaging was the highly unusual one of cutting prices.

That certainly went against the grain of a manufacturer that had led the pack in construction equipment for fifty years and that had always commanded premium rates for quality and service. But as an industry analyst told *Fortune*'s Ronald Henkoff, "They had the choice of losing money or losing markets, and they chose to lose money." In other words, Cat chose to secure its long-term account position, even though it cost in the short run.

Cost the firm it did—just shy of $1 *billion* between 1982 and 1984. But at the end of that parched period, with both the recession and labor troubles lifting, the company managed not only to rebound in share points but to regain its traditional hold on the mining and construction markets—including the Large Accounts that had always paid its bills. Echoing the opinion of many observers, Henkoff wrote that the Peoria company's turnaround made it "an exemplar for American industry."

We're not recommending a markets-first, profits-next strategy. In some situations that could be disastrous. What we're saying is that *any* effective strategy has to look to the consistent management of Large Accounts way beyond this quota period or this fiscal year.

STRATEGY OF SCALE AND YOUR ROI

How far beyond? How many quarters into the future should you peer as you set up a Large Account strategy?

Forget about quarters. If we're talking about the survival of your business, we have to be talking in terms of years. The clients who attend our LAMP seminars set strategies with *at least* a one-year time frame; we encourage them to plan three years out. It takes that long for major projects to bear fruit. And management of a Large Account is definitely major.

Admittedly, this is unusually long range. Most businesses set "strategies" for no more than a year in advance. "Here's our 1989 West Coast marketing plan." "What's the second-half Betco

Group forecast?" But in the future-shock world we all inhabit, that's shortsighted.

Industry leaders know this. When Caterpillar was still bobbing in red ink back in 1982, its managers decided to invest $1.2 billion in a factory modernization that they believed would dramatically cut production and inventory costs. The return on that investment wasn't expected until the early 1990s—at least *eight years* down the road—yet Cat's managers took the calculated risk because the anticipated ROI was so great. Their regained industry position is already proving that they were right.

Or ask yourself this question: "Which companies, right now, are best positioned to reap the trade benefits of Europe 1992?" *Not* the firms that just started thinking about a united Europe this year. The winners-to-be in the new Common Market have been busy for a decade or more charting French demographics, talking to Dutch CEOs, bringing their lawyers up to speed on Italian tariffs. This has cost time and money, sure. But the potential return, long term, makes it worth it.

Underlying our entire approach to business is the conviction that setting strategies is an *investment*. Just as is true with regard to a plant modernization or a revamped accounting system, the ROI on setting strategies may not be immediate. But just as with these more conventional investments, if the potential is high enough, you take the gamble. And nothing in business today has a higher potential return than long-term investment in Large Accounts.

FROM ACCOUNT STRATEGY TO
BUSINESS STRATEGY

What do a couple of professional salesman know about such arcane boardroom topics as lower production costs and ROI? Everything.

We're not patting ourselves on the backs. We're directing your attention to a simple fact that everyone learns in Economics 101, but that modern businesses tend to lose sight of in a forest of Laffer curves and chi-square analyses.

Robert Louis Stevenson phrased it well: "Everyone lives by selling something." Your economics professor may have put it a little differently when she talked about market price and consumer sovereignty. But both were getting at the same truth. In a competitive, free-market economy, *selling goods* is the engine that drives the system, and the person who buys, or doesn't buy, a company's goods is the ultimate arbiter of whether the business sinks or swims. Investment bankers and systems analysts aside, if a company loses its customers, it bites the dust.

Because we understand the central importance of the customer (Adam Smith would have called it "the market"), we define "account" strategy in the broadest possible way. Account management has got to be more than a "sales" function; because your "external assets" directly affect revenue and profit, account strategy is necessarily a *business* strategy. We address this book, with confidence and without apology, to the managers of every company that lives by sales—which is to say every company that has a pulse. The Large Account Management Process is the only holistic approach to accounts on the market today. It's the only system that insists on the integration of account management with the business at large, so that the revenue stream translates into profit.

The last time we checked our Adam Smith, that was what doing business was all about.

|3|

LAMP
Strategy Workshops:
A User's Guide

The operational uniqueness of this book—the feature that puts it
in an entirely different league from other so-called management
guides—is that its pragmatic utility is *built in*. We don't merely
suggest that you "ought" to perform such-and-such an information analysis on your accounts; we give you the precise means to
do so in a series of Strategy Workshops. As you become familiar
with our methodology, these Workshops will enable you to apply
LAMP analysis to your *own* Large Accounts right away, so that
the strategies you set will have an impact, immediate and pragmatic, on your business.

The Workshops are decidedly "user friendly." You can work
through this "portable" LAMP program with no more tools than a
notebook and some pencils. But to reap the greatest benefits that
you can from the process, we encourage you to remember three
things: teamwork, customer input, and what we call, quite
bluntly, the "sweat factor."

THE TEAM APPROACH

LAMP analyses that work come out of creative thinking by account *teams*—that is, by groups of individuals who have personal
stakes in an account's growth and stability. Therefore, as you

begin this program, one of the first steps you should take is to start considering which members of your organization do, can, or should affect the management of given Large Accounts. The more input you have from these people, the more reliable your analyses will be.

We can't tell you which members of your organization should or shouldn't be on a given account management team. But we can tell you, with a certainty born of long experience, that the most effective Large Account strategies are created, synergistically, by small groups—groups where *every* member is committed to the account's long-term success.

In our LAMP programs, a typical team might be composed of the salespeople directly responsible for the business being targeted, their branch or division sales manager, and representatives from such areas as marketing, design, engineering, and customer service—in other words, those who *support* the account. But that's only one of innumerable team patterns. When a giant corporation identifies another giant as a Large Account, there might be fifty or sixty people in the selling organization who are, directly or indirectly, targeting that business. Product development people, service people, market research people— folks from any of these areas and from many more might be useful members of an account "team." There's no magic configuration, in terms either of size or of the members' "function." The composition of teams is less important, we've discovered repeatedly, than the commitment of team members to the account's success.

That commitment doesn't have to be made visible every Wednesday morning at ten o'clock. In fact, rarely do all members of an account management team get together at the same time to plan a strategy. Team "membership," as we define it, is indicated not by names on a list or bodies in a room, but by the willingness of all those who affect the account to provide information and analysis whenever it's needed to the team members who most frequently interact with the customer.

The obvious value of a team approach is synergy: More neurons flash in a group of six than you can possibly get from a single brain. In addition, a team approach helps to establish a sense of shared responsibility without which no Large Account strategy can be implemented. Often it also improves the customer's responsiveness. In the famous Hawthorne plant studies in the 1930s, researchers discovered the mere fact that managers were paying attention to their workers made the workers more responsive to production demands. Get six people paying attention to the Murdock account, and Murdock gets the message loud and clear: His business matters to your firm.

The only way he'll *really* get that message, though, is when *senior managers* from your organization, as well as the more predictable sales representatives and account managers, visibly pay attention to the account. Because Large Accounts are external assets, it's essential that top-level managers be involved in setting strategies for managing them. In our LAMP programs that's a contractual given: We won't conduct a workshop for a client unless general management agrees to participate along with the sales force, and also agrees that their ongoing involvement is essential to the handling of their Large Accounts.

Put that principle into effect right now as you work through this book. Since LAMP is a *business* operations system, be sure that the decision makers at the business level—not just the sales level—are involved.

INVOLVING THE CUSTOMER

There's an old saying that if you really want to know what business you're in, don't ask your marketing people. Ask your customers.

The comment is too hard on marketing people—it's neither wise nor realistic to ignore them—but it's right on target regarding the customer. Businesses that expect to stay alive have got to ask their customers, on a frequent basis, not only "what business they're in" but also how they're doing in that business—and how they can do better for the customer.

We make this truth a central feature of LAMP analysis by recommending, at the beginning of the program, that you make people in the Large Account itself, as well as people in your own organization, part of the account planning team. It sounds revolutionary, and it is. It's also no more than common sense. After all, who knows more about the problems of the Murdock organization than Murdock's own people? If you're going to commit as a company to the more effective management of their business, it makes perfect sense regularly to ask their people where they're hurting, so you can devise mutually beneficial solutions. In fact, it's self-defeating not to.

It's unrealistic, we realize, to suppose that Murdock people will make themselves available, say, once a week for a strategy session with your account team. But it's not unrealistic to expect that the Murdock organization will be receptive to your questions, and willing to provide you input, *as the need for it arises*, about how you can serve their needs better. That's teamwork too, and what we're really suggesting is that in the best account teams, the customer becomes both resource and partner.

There are models of the "extended team" approach we're recommending. One of the most successful is Coca-Cola's customer advisory boards, composed of Coke bottlers and customers who, once or twice a year, meet in Atlanta to provide feedback to the home office. Another is the Apple company's user groups, composed of the computer firm's oldest and most reliable customers—in effect, the company's Large Accounts, whose input can dramatically affect Apple strategy. The cooperative vendor-customer relationship that these groups typify is exactly what we're recommending for Large Account planning.

THE SWEAT FACTOR

We've said that you'll be "working," not "reading," the process. The distinction is not semantics: This book is *work*. It's no summer vacation beach read or frequent flyer skimmer. There's no reason it should be. You've paid good money for it. You have a right to expect it will deliver for you, and not just with nineteenth-hole chitchat. It *will* deliver—but only if you put in the time.

You deserve an honest idea of what to expect. Maybe you're one of the lucky thousands who've attended sales training seminars where you're promised 132 "fresh perspectives" on your profession. What you get is the same old dogs and same tired ponies, and not even the salad is fresh. This isn't that. We promise you results, in your Large Accounts and in your bottom line, and we promise you that you'll sweat for them.

Up till now we've been speaking about accounts in the plural. Get some pencils and a large spiral notebook. You're about to select one account as your first target for Large Account Management.

PART II

Situation Appraisal

‖4‖

Targeting
Your Large Account

Even though you'll eventually apply LAMP analysis to all your major accounts, one of them has to come first. If your business is at all like ours, or like those of our corporate clients, you'll have several candidates to choose from. Which is best?

One answer is to start at the top: Select for your initial LAMP analysis the account that brings your company the most revenue. There's nothing wrong with that; many of our clients start there. But it's not your only sound option.

We advise you to consider more than revenue. LAMP brings clarity into chaos by helping businesses better organize their information. For this reason, the process is particularly valuable when your information is unclear—where, in spite of good revenue, you feel confused about where the account is going. Gut feelings of uncertainty should be taken seriously. Therefore, we recommend that you target first one of your gray-area, something's-off accounts. Not only will you get more out of working a "gray" account, but this is the type of account where you *need* it most. As Loose Cannon George's fellow managers found out, it's painfully easy to find yourself behind the eight ball when you ignore your sense that "something" is wrong.

"PREVENTIVE DIAGNOSIS"

Identifying a Large Account that is "due" for LAMP analysis means bringing to the surface hidden problems *before* they become overwhelming. To help you perform this kind of "preventive diagnosis," we suggest you ask yourself these questions:

1. *Is there any inconsistency in your account planning, over geography or over time?* Do you and your company have a consistent plan for handling this Large Account's various regional (or international) business units? Do you understand how the units fit together? Or do the organizational and purchasing structures of the parent account sometimes seem like impenetrable labyrinths? What about time? Does your account planning show a purposeful evolution from one year to the next? Or is each quarter's "plan" an entirely new species?

2. *Do your account strategies ever fail to impact, positively and indisputably, on your company's revenues and profit?* What's the perceived link between your strategies and the money you're making from the account? Can you document that link, or are you guessing? Do you have a clear understanding of how the account got to be "large"? Or did it "just get that way" by momentum? Perhaps most important of all, do the strategies that you adopt for this customer impact positively on his or her revenue? If the relationship you've established so far isn't showing up on the *customer's* bottom line, he or she is a top candidate for LAMP analysis.

3. *Do you ever wonder about the reliability of your company's system for reviewing and measuring account plans?* If an account plan is working (or not working), how early does your company know it? How frequently, and in how disciplined a fashion, do you track progress on individual objectives for this Large Account? If a given goal proves unrealistic, can you "regroup and reset" quickly? Or are you sometimes left hanging, like George's colleagues, planning midcourse corrections too late?

4. *Do you ever lack the budget to do the job?* Is there a reasonable degree of congruity between your account plans and the re-

sources that they require? Does your company's top management understand that this Large Account is critical not just to your success, but to the success of the firm? Are you usually able to convince them that the expected return on investment from this account justifies spending resources up front? Or are you often a day late and a dollar short?

5. *Are you insecure in your position?* Do you feel confident that you understand this Large Account and your place in it as "external" manager? Do you know who makes decisions, and on what grounds? Have you fully explored sales possibilities in the account beyond those currently on the table? What about the competition? How firm is your position compared to theirs? And—most important of all—do you know how decision makers in the Large Account feel about *your* place in their business? If you're not sure what they feel—or if you're unsure about any other aspect of your position—mark this up as a major gray area.

We urge you to be brutally honest in your responses to these diagnostic questions and to trust your instincts as well as your head. Isolate those Large Accounts where you are uncertain about your position. Then select one to work through the process first.

GATHERING INFORMATION: FOCUS ON THE USABLE

Good account strategies aren't set in a vacuum. They are by definition the effective management of *information*. The better the information, the better the strategy. Therefore, once you've selected your first target, you need to gather account data.

We realize that when you heard the phrase "gather data," your eyes immediately glazed over. You've probably done your share of "annual account plans" that weigh half as much as the Manhattan phone book. That's not what we're getting at. We at Miller Heiman recognize the uselessness of most account data. We're urging you to put the "More Is Better" philosophy in the shredder where it belongs, and concentrate on gathering information you can *use*.

To help you separate the garbage from the gems, we propose two guidelines:

1. Look for information that relates to *what you sell customers*.
2. Look for information regarding *trends in customers' businesses*.

The first tip is mere common sense—although you wouldn't know that from the heft of those phone-book account plans. Your planners can tally up the most sophisticated customer- and industry-specific data in the world, but if it doesn't relate to the specific relationship you want to establish with the customer, it's like what the politician once said about his polyglot opponent: "Knows six languages and has nothing to say." "Usable" means usable for *your* sales.

The second tip is less obvious. Look for information that tells you where your customers are going—and where they think they could be going, given current trends. The key to usability here is that word "trends." Any information you can pull together about *changes* in your accounts' business environment, about threats to their position from *their* competitors, about the *direction* their businesses are taking, about their "mission"—all these things can help you devise a strategy that ties in with, and perhaps complements, *their* strategic concerns. "Usable" is what makes you useful to your customers.

Here's an example from our own business. A couple of years ago, doing research on one of our largest clients, we discovered two critical facts. One, their *profits* were down. Two, their anticipated growth was *offshore*.

We found plenty more facts, of course. But to the Miller Heiman team that was setting strategies for this Large Account, we emphasized the importance of these two. Both told us something about change in the customer's environment: Clearly, profits and international expansion were "trend" issues. At the same time, both related to *our* business. Our programs could help increase the customer's sales productivity and thus profits, and we saw a new market opening for us in the firm's international group. Two perfectly *usable* bits of account data.

WHERE TO FIND IT: FIVE SOURCES

Where do you find such information? Here's where we advise you to look:

1. Your own sales data. This includes both "past" and "future" data. You want to know what you've sold this account in the past two or three years, broken down preferably by *product line* and by which *division* (plant, branch, business unit) of the account actually did the business with your company. You also want to know what you're likely to sell the account in the immediate future, or what your forecasts say you will. Later in the book we'll present a reality-testing method for such forecasts; now you just want to have on hand your best current estimate of future sales.

2. The account's reports. This means, minimally, its latest annual report. It could also include the firm's 10K report, annual reports from the past two or three years, recent quarterly reports, promotional brochures, and product and service literature. These will provide you with this customer's view of its own position— something you *must* understand when setting strategies.

If your targeted Large Account is a private company, the financial data may not be easy to come by. But even private firms issue advertising, promotional, and informational literature that can give you a handle on how they see themselves. The more you have, the clearer the picture.

3. Investment opinions. If you're dealing with a public company, assessments of its stock's viability can provide a useful "health check." Such opinions may come from television commentators, from newspaper reports, and from investment firms' own published literature.

4. The print media. We recommend that your team assign one person to spend a day in the local university or public library, reading recently published articles on your Large Account *and* on its industry, then photocopying four or five articles that focus on industry changes and trends. If your people haven't logged any library time since college, don't panic. You can get a good deal of basic information from the *Standard & Poor's* and *Moody's* indexes. In addition, most libraries today subscribe to computer indexing services, which make researching a customer much easier than it was in the old *Reader's Guide* days.

Have your researcher ask the reference librarian for *InfoTrac*, *Predicast*, the *Business Collection*, or the *Business Index*. These indexes will steer him or her to articles in the general press (*New York Times*, *Wall Street Journal*), the business press (*Forbes*, *Business Week*, *Fortune*), and the trade press (everything from *Industry Week* to *Milk and Liquid Food Transporter Monthly*).

5. *People in the Large Account.* Insiders again. Ask *them* about what you find in the press. As you'll see, this is a technique that we'll be recommending throughout the process. It's especially valuable at the outset. Add to your knowledge of the account, and get a fix on where *they* think they are, by asking the people you're selling to directly, "What are your most pressing trends and issues?"

You may not know anyone in the Large Account who can give you this kind of information, or there may be no one you feel comfortable enough to ask for it. If that's the case, this is the time to start developing such a contact. We'll be speaking later about Strategic Coaches as critical resources. As a preliminary step in developing a Strategic Coach, try to identify at least one person in the customer's organization who (a) has broad knowledge of how the company operates and (b) has a personal interest in doing business with your firm. Information obtained from such a person can be an invaluable check on other information.

In addition to seeking out such allies, we also urge you to contact account people with whom you *don't* feel comfortable. This is important as a reality check, and also as a way of bringing to the surface information that you should hear but might not want to. Although backing away from unpleasant information is common and understandable, it's never smart, because it short-changes you right at the outset—and frequently short-circuits your strategy.

DOING THE SPADEWORK

We recommend that the information you pull together be made available to each team member *before* you begin setting strategy—in other words, before you begin the next chapter. This doesn't mean everybody should memorize every line in the Large Account's financial report. It does mean that everybody on your account team should know how your company is currently positioned with the account, how the account is currently positioned in the business environment, and what issues and trends are likely to affect the way you and this customer work together.

This isn't finger-wagging. We speak from painful experience. In our LAMP workshops, we ask each team to do this basic "spadework" on its Large Account weeks before beginning the program. Trying to conduct a strategy analysis when the team has not done this "boring," "academic," up-front work is like trying to plant a seed in solid granite. Frankly, that's a waste of our time and the client's money.

On one occasion a few months ago, for example, we had just begun a LAMP workshop for a large machine parts company when it became painfully obvious that the account team had not done the necessary research on the customer. The targeted Large Account was the resource development ministry of a foreign government. The ministry, which was engaged in a major road construction project, had purchased thousands of parts from the U.S. firm over several years, yet for some reason on this deal negotiations had stalled: Key players in the foreign ministry had become inaccessible, and the nature of the project itself seemed ill defined. As one exasperated account manager confessed to us, "We're not even sure where the damn road is being built."

With this poor a handle on the account, we explained to the team, it was virtually impossible to perform effective analysis. So, rather than tie up two days of everybody's schedule in fruitless guesswork, we canceled the program on the spot. We lost money on that decision, but we got it back later when the client returned, this time well prepared, and the analysis ran as it was designed to.

To reiterate what we said earlier, this book is not vacation reading. It's hard work. We don't apologize for that, because it's worth it. Just *how* worth it you're about to find out.

‖5‖

Charter Statement

You'll begin by drafting a document we call the Charter Statement. Like a corporate mission statement, this document will define the basic direction of your business activity. Unlike a mission statement, however, the Charter Statement will focus exclusively on a single account. Indeed, it will focus even more narrowly on one *portion* of your targeted Large Account for which your team can most effectively set a strategy.

We ask you to do this at the outset because in setting strategies, account teams often try to target too broad a segment of their chosen account, or they try to sell their products and services to the wrong segment, or—worst of all—they don't think about "segments" at all, and try to inhale the entire account at one shot. The inevitable results are loss of focus and foggy strategies.

A sound Charter Statement helps them, and it will help you, avoid these problems. The document states three things about the account:

- What portion of the Large Account you are selling to. We call this portion your *field of play.*
- *What* you're going to sell the customer.
- The *contribution* that you can make to the *customer's* business.

ONE ARM AT A TIME

Why should you focus on a limited, designated field of play within your targeted Large Account?

Consider the case of one of our clients—a leading-edge data service company that provides credit information to the financial and insurance industries. One of its most lucrative accounts is American Express; the account brought in nearly eight figures in revenue last year. But "American Express" is not a uniform entity. It's composed of five major subsidiaries: Travel Related Services, IDS Financial Services, Shearson Lehman Hutton, American Express Bank, and the recently formed AMEX Information Services. Each of these subsidiaries is in turn a huge, multiarmed concern employing thousands of people worldwide. TRS alone manages businesses in cards and traveler's checks, data-based services, direct marketing, merchandising, and publishing. Nobody sells—nobody *could* sell—to all these businesses in the same way or with the same account strategy. Trying to do so would be confusing and self-destructive. So when our client targets "the AMEX account," it practices what Tom Peters and Bob Waterman call "chunking," setting one strategy for IDS, one for Shearson, and so on. It's *got* to start by asking "Which AMEX?"

The AMEX case is hardly unique. Most companies today grow by subdividing. Even the ones that say they're sticking to the knitting tend to define knitting in broad, diversified terms. Johnson & Johnson, for example, now sells not just its traditional Band-Aids and baby products but analgesics, contraceptives, mouthwash, diapers, and shampoo—with a different management structure for each one. The typical Large Account today resembles what a friend of ours calls the corporate octopus.

You can't shake all eight arms of an octopus at once (even if you wanted to), and you can't sell to a corporate octopus in its entirety. That's why the first step in the Large Account Management Process is to define a manageable field of play.

AVOIDING THE "VAPORWARE" TRAP

The second step is to decide *what* you should be placing with this customer in this field of play. This is a more subtle process than merely itemizing your products and services. Presenting your customers with a laundry list implies that you've got minimal interest in their needs and that you'll sell anything to anybody, any time. Selling effectively to Large Accounts means reviewing what you've sold them in the past, distinguishing the good sales from the bad ones (we've all had our share of bad ones), and discovering which of the many items in your product or service line have a genuine fit to each customer's needs. Sometimes it also means rewriting the "menu" you can offer customers based not on what you've been selling them but on that product/ need fit.

We have run LAMP programs for several major suppliers of information systems—systems that include hardware, software, and a vast array of support services. At a recent program, while account teams from one of these companies were trying to thrash out a Charter Statement, a district sales manager said in frustration, "You know, narrowing things down is a tricky business. We could probably find a reason to sell this account everything our company makes. Software, hardware, vaporware."

Laughter from his colleagues let us know that "vaporware" was an inside joke. We asked what it meant.

The district manager explained. "It's company code for 'total solution' selling. 'Promises, promises.' When a customer knows zip about computers, and when he doesn't really know what he needs, you can sell him on almost any package—convince him that it will do everything and anything. 'Our systems are infinitely expandable to any configuration.' The Spandex pitch. Solid as vapor."

"What happens when he finds out you've oversold him?" we wanted to know. "Does the vaporware sale ever come back to haunt you?"

Laughter again. "Every time," the manager admitted. "We've all gotten stung selling vaporware. In the long run it's much smarter to be specific."

Our point exactly, we acknowledged—and not just in the software/hardware game. We're firmly on the side of "solution selling," but true solutions are the answers to *specific* problems, and no product or service, no matter how "expandable," solves *all* problems. Even Spandex snaps if you stretch it too far—half the time right back in your face.

WHAT'S IN IT FOR THE CUSTOMER?

Identifying which of your products or services really tie in to your customer's problems leads directly to the final step of the Charter Statement: determining what *contribution* you can make to your customer's business.

His or her business. Not yours. To effectively manage a Large Account, you've got to see "contribution" through the customer's eyes, and deliver value that enhances his or her bottom line.

This is neither natural nor easy. When you're selling what you believe to be a good product, it's natural to assess its value "from the inside": *Our* PC 421 has so many megabytes of memory, *we* provide the fastest delivery in the East, and so on. But, as Adam Smith pointed out two hundred years ago, a market system doesn't tolerate "natural" value: A product's value is what you can get for it, and that is determined, almost exclusively, by *what customers think it can do for them*. That's why it's essential to reverse the "natural" order of vendor thinking and state value from the account's point of view.

In the Strategy Workshop you'll try in a moment, we'll show you, in practical terms, how to do this. First let's look at some examples of Charter Statements, to illustrate how the three parts lock together.

HONING IT DOWN

Few LAMP teams draft a perfect Charter Statement right off the bat. Typically, the first draft is so "vaporous" that it's hard to tell, from the written statement, exactly what the team sells and to whom. Some of them read like the TV astrologer's promise to deliver "the answer" to a question no one has asked.

One example from a recent program will illustrate how these vague statements are honed down into usable documents. The team was five managers from an electronics company. Their first-draft Charter Statement read like this:

> We sell electronics solutions to "General Aviation" that give them state-of-the-art testing capabilities.

Not a bad start. You have a who (General Aviation), a what (electronics solutions), and a contribution (state-of-the-art testing capabilities). But does it stand up, as a reliable Charter Statement, to close inspection? No—on at least four counts:

First, the field of play is not well defined. The company that we're calling General Aviation is in fact a six-division multinational—a corporate octopus that can't be analyzed as a whole.

Second, "electronics solutions" says very little. It's better than the smoke-in-your-eyes "total solutions," but not much. This first draft of the Statement fails to spell out what specific problems are being addressed by the seller's "solutions."

Third, the "contribution" is also vaguely defined. "State-of-the-art testing capabilities" is, like "solutions," a basket term. It could refer not only to electronics but to anything from plastics to personnel. It's even difficult to tell from this statement what specific business the account team is in. That's the top of the slippery slope into Vaporware Valley.

Fourth, the "contribution" is spelled out backward. It says what the seller finds of value, *not* the value the firm can bring to the customer. This may seem like a merely verbal distinction. Our experience shows that it's not. A good Charter Statement phrases the contribution *as it's seen by the customer.* The version given here doesn't tell us why General Aviation would even *want* "state-of-the-art testing."

When we made these observations to the team members, they grumbled their way back to the drawing board. The second draft was a little sharper, the third even better, and by the fourth round and the fifteenth cup of coffee, they came up with this final Charter Statement:

> We provide General Aviation's Aerospace Division with the most accurate electronics testing equipment on the market, so that they can improve their quality control and thus maintain their competitive advantage.

Vaporware out, customer value in. The Charter Statement now defines which segment of the Large Account is being targeted (the Aerospace Division), precisely what's being sold (electronics testing *equipment*), and the bottom-line value for the customer (improved quality control and competitiveness). When the team asked for our assessment of this final version, we responded with one word: "Perfect."

It doesn't always work out this way. Sometimes, even after four drafts, you still seem no closer to wrestling down the octopus than you were before the first cup of coffee. Typically, there are two reasons why this happens. Either you lack essential information about the Large Account that will enable you to draft an effective charter, or the team members who are wrestling with the statement view the Large Account itself in different ways.

We've already mentioned an example of the first scenario: The account team from the machine parts company that tried to deal, without adequate information, with a foreign government. And we mentioned how their fog was dispelled: The account team, unable to draft a Charter Statement, went back to find essential information, and came back with a clear "who," "what," and "why."

We witnessed the second scenario at a recent LAMP workshop where the client was a huge insurance company. The targeted account was another huge company—a multidivision consumer products firm. Ten minutes into the Charter Statement portion of the workshop, it became obvious that the account team was at loggerheads. Half the team members worked in the pensions "segment" of this Large Account, while the other half specialized in claims and benefits. So it wasn't Company A targeting Company B; it was two separate segments of the insurer firm targeting two separate segments of the consumer products firm. Naturally there was confusion.

The confusion was dispelled quickly and intelligently by an account manager who said, "Why don't we make like an amoeba and divide?" They did just that, forming two teams, each with its own responsibility and field of play. And out of it came *two* clear Charter Statements.

You'll understand these problems more concretely, and you'll see concretely how they can be overcome, as you apply the concepts we've just laid out to your business. It's time to start work on your Large Account, in the first of our Strategy Workshops.

One warning. It's tempting, when you work in a group, to slip into one-upmanship and point-scoring. Resist that temptation. In this and all subsequent Workshops, there are no right or wrong answers. The goal is not to draft the one "correct" strategy (there ain't no such animal), or even to achieve complete agreement. It's to work, consensus fashion, toward a common goal: a clearer understanding, and thus better management, of the account.

STRATEGY WORKSHOP 1: CHARTER STATEMENT

Step 1. Define your field of play.

You've chosen the Large Account you're going to set your first strategy for. Now determine which *portion* of that account your team can realistically manage. Write down the heading "Charter Statement" on a blank page of your notebook; under it define your field of play. It may be a division, a territory, a subsidiary, a department, or some other entity. It should *not* be the entire octopus.

To help you decide whether the piece of business you're eyeing is a manageable "chunk," ask yourself these questions:

• *Information.* Do we have enough information to set a strategy for this segment of the Large Account? How much do we currently understand about the internal organization of the account? About the people responsible for approving sales? About the account's problems, threats, and opportunities? About the industry of which it's a part? If you feel less than confident about your understanding of the account in any of these critical areas, gather more information before you proceed.

• *Responsibility.* In targeting this field of play, are we within our own area of responsibility, or are we infringing on somebody else's? Suppose your organization markets internationally. As part of a North American account team, you might not be well positioned to set strategy for the Pacific Rim market; the Asian operations sector would be positioned better. This doesn't mean that a North American team should never seek to tap a Korean market; it means that tapping such a market effectively would mean cooperation between the American and Asian sectors, to determine who should be responsible for which actions.

• *Team.* Are you sure that every member of the account team agrees about the value of this segment? No account strategy has a chance unless its drafters buy into its potential, and the only way to ensure that is for each member of the team to see a "win" in the ongoing development of account business. For a field representative, the win might be the satisfaction of closing a major deal; for her manager, it might be a boost in sales revenues. A marketing manager might see the Large Account as an opportunity to carve out a lucrative niche; an operations officer might see potential boosts in profit. The nature of the wins is not important. But everyone on your team, on some level, has got to see a personal plus in better business from this account.

• *Priority.* Does this portion of the Large Account have high priority in terms of your current position and future sales potential? We've urged you to target an account where something is "off." We *don't* mean the billion-dollar pie-in-the-sky customer where you barely have a foot in the door. You should be focusing on a piece of good business that strategy can make better and more reliable. If it's not already bringing you solid revenue, by definition it's not a Large Account.

• *Position.* We've stressed not biting off more than you can chew. Don't bite off too little either. Can you be positioned with a broader segment of the account? For example, if you now sell to only one of the Geoplex Company's ten plants, is it feasible that you could reach all ten? If you sell to Boston, can you cover New England? Can you move from division to group, or from group to corporate? Think about where your field of play might be broadened over the next one to three years.

In using these questions, some teams discover, as our insurance company client discovered, that they have to "make like an amoeba and divide." Others find they're so ignorant of the account situation that they need more research before they can even begin. And many teams discover that their original field of play is too wide. It's not the Aerospace Division after all; it's that division's circuit board subsidiary. Use the questions to discover your own uncertainties and, if necessary, adjust your definition of "field of play."

Step 2. Review your sales history in this field of play.

Now define the Charter Statement's "what." Because one guide to the present is the past, take a few minutes to review the various "whats" that your company has already placed with this account. To summarize your current position in the account, briefly write down the following:

- Major sales *victories* in the account—especially those closed in the last two or three years.
- *Sales in progress* but still to be closed.
- Any *problems or concerns*—yours or the customer's— regarding these still-pending sales.
- Past *losses* to the competition, with the reasons that each one went bad.
- Current *opportunities* in the account—"current" being defined as one to three years out.

You don't need to write a tome on these items. A total of one page should be sufficient to give you a general feel for how you've been doing.

Step 3. Define what you'll sell them.

Now bring the picture into the present, by writing down what you're currently trying to sell. Products, services, programs, contracts—whichever of your possible "whats" fit *this* field of play. Questions to help your thinking:

- Are you trying to place too many *different* products or services with them? Is the account's interest as diversified as your menu, or more focused? Would it make sense to narrow your scope and exploit more fully the areas in which you've been most successful?

• On the other hand, have you been too *narrow*, too conservative, in your dealings with this account? Are there signals in the buying organization that it's ready to consider a broader selection of your products or services? If so, which other segments of the customer's company should you be looking to for business? Which other segment of *your* company should be involved in developing this business?

• Finally, have you looked down the road? Based on your company's recent history with this account, what new business opportunities might be developed with it in the next year? The next three? The next ten?

With these questions in mind, make appropriate revisions in the "what" section of your Charter Statement. Ideally, your Charter Statement should indicate not only what you successfully place with this account now, but what it's likely you can place in the near future.

Step 4. Define the contribution you make to their business.

Now write down, from the *account's* point of view, what value you bring to their business. This is always the trickiest part of the Charter Statement—and the part that makes it or breaks it. Your goal is to perceive your "contribution" as the customer will perceive it; that's the only way you'll know it *is* a contribution. To determine whether this account will benefit by doing business with you, ask:

• Does the actual *phrasing* of your contribution statement put the emphasis on the customer's perception?

Here's a sample vendor-centered phrasing:

We'll sell them our System B12 so they'll save money on inventory costs.

Here's the same contribution statement but phrased from the account's point of view:

We'll help them save on inventory costs by using our System B12.

The distinction is subtle but essential. Only the second version really answers the question "What's in it for the account?" Only this phrasing speaks to the client's (perhaps unspoken) question, "Why should I spend money on the B12?"

• Does (or can) your contribution deliver *profit-oriented* results to this customer? Can it help the account increase *its* productivity, boost *its* sales, or lower *its* costs? In other words, does the "value" you're adding really affect the account's bottom line? If you can't document that this is so, you may not be making as valid a contribution as you think you are. We'll say more about this later in the book, but here's the basic point: The only "added values" your customers really want are those that help them improve their *own* business positions.

Step 5. Draft your Charter Statement.

Now bring together all that you've identified into a draft of your Charter Statement. Team members should reach consensus on the wording of this statement, and it should clearly define the field of play, the products or services you sell, and the contribution/value added for the account's business. The Charter Statement template we give our clients looks like this:

We supply _____ (products, lines, services, etc.) to _____ (field of play: division, group, subsidiary, etc.) that _____ (contribution: value you'll add to account's business).

This is only a template. Modify it as you see fit. Just be sure the wording of the Charter Statement clearly defines the "who," "what," and "why."

Step 6. Test this Charter Statement.

To test your draft Charter Statement against reality, we suggest that you ask yourself these questions:

• *Would a stranger understand this Charter Statement without a great deal of technical explanation?* We don't mean Joe Doofus off the street, but a reasonably awake, business-savvy individual who doesn't happen to know your business or your industry. An intelligent but uninformed stranger should be able to read your Statement and know instantly what you're trying to sell and to whom. If he can't, the wording may be vague or too technical. Revise as needed.

• *Would your account recognize your company from this Charter Statement?* A good Charter Statement defines very precisely the business relationship between you and the account. If people at the account wouldn't be able to "see" you in the Statement—if they couldn't distinguish you in this statement from your competitors—then either you're not clearly differentiated from other vendors or you haven't yet defined clearly enough—to the customer—the special value that you're bringing to his or her business. Maybe you haven't even defined it for yourself. We address this problem in more detail in the next chapter.

THE ACID TEST OF THE CHARTER STATEMENT

One final question to assess Charter Statement validity. Would you *show this document* to the customer? We know it's an unusual idea. Few companies are so market-driven that they're ready to include the customer in strategy sessions. But as we pointed out in chapter 3, "involving the customer" is a key ingredient of LAMP analysis.

For this reason, the "acid test" of your Statement is very simple: Show it to your customer and ask what he or she thinks. If the customer doesn't recognize his or her company's self-interest in the document, your team has got more work to do.

Former New York mayor Ed Koch wasn't everybody's idea of the perfect public official. But he got one thing right. When he wanted to know how his "customers" saw his work, he didn't hedge. He blurted out, "How'm I doing?" A politician's tactic? Maybe so. But it's not a bad way to find out what folks will "buy" and what they won't. Like him or not, Ed did get elected three times.

A "FINAL" DRAFT

Now that you've run your Charter Statement past our test questions, write down a "final" draft version. We put the word in quotes for a reason. The Charter Statement you've put together in this first Strategy Workshop is as close to final as you can get *now*. But as you work your way through the process in other workshops, you'll find aspects of the Statement that no longer seem to work, and you'll have to go back and revise. Since the secret of LAMP's success is *dynamic* analysis, it would be strange if this didn't happen.

So put the "final" draft of your Charter Statement aside for now, and don't worry if it doesn't seem "perfect." We're going to turn to a detailed analysis of your account situation. By the time you finish this analysis, you'll have at your disposal a rich store of newly-surfaced information. With this new information, not only will you be able to revise your draft Charter Statement; but you'll be able to begin designing your first strategy.

| 6 |

Moving Up the Buy-Sell Hierarchy: Levels of Business Relationship

Having an account means having a relationship, and a business relationship, no less than a personal one, can be strongly forged and enduring or as flimsy as a short-lived affair. In this chapter we present a unique relational model, the concept of the buy-sell hierarchy, to help you create more lasting business associations. We present this concept at some length because it's a prerequisite for the situation appraisal you'll be performing in the next three chapters.

As you can see from the diagram that follows, the hierarchy of buy-sell relationships is divided into five levels. We'll describe each of these levels in detail. But let's start with some general observations.

First, the hierarchy is a visual metaphor for your *position* with an account. Given what we've said about strategy and position, you can conclude that understanding the level of your business relationship—that is, knowing where you are in the hierarchy— is an indispensable piece of account information.

Second, it's not you, but your *customer*, who decides at what level you're positioned. There's some irony here. We'll be recommending that you "work your way up" the buy-sell hierarchy; yet it's your customer who decides how successfully you do this. The

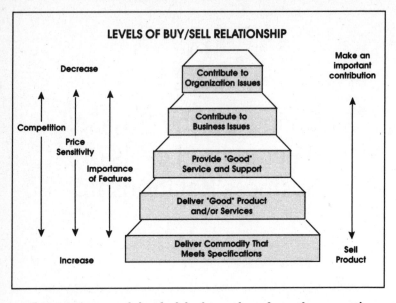

LEVELS OF BUY/SELL RELATIONSHIP

Decrease

Competition

Price Sensitivity

Importance of Features

Increase

Make an important contribution

Contribute to Organization Issues

Contribute to Business Issues

Provide "Good" Service and Support

Deliver "Good" Product and/or Services

Deliver Commodity That Meets Specifications

Sell Product

descriptions at each level of the hierarchy refer to the *account's* assessment of your position.

Third, the levels of the buy-sell hierarchy should be understood not as discrete steps or plateaus but as positions along a continuum. Your customer will probably have a pretty solid sense of where you're positioned, but it may not be quantifiable: No magic signal will inform him or her that you've just moved from level 2 to level 3.

Don't worry now about the material on either side of the hierarchy diagram; we'll explain it later in the chapter. Let's start by looking at the bottom level.

LEVEL 1: COMMODITIES

At the first, and lowest, level of business relationship, you are seen as the supplier of a commodity. It's easy to get positioned at this level, but there's no leverage here for establishing long-term relationships. Here's why.

In the New York and Chicago futures markets, a commodity is something traded in bulk, with no regard for special features or added value. Oats, gold, crude oil, gypsum, pork bellies: These very different products have one thing in common. They've got to meet minimum standards, but there's virtually no competition with regard to quality beyond those standards. One supplier's East Texas crude is pretty much the same as the next supplier's. One producer's 24 karat gold is indistinguishable from that of the competition. Availability and (most important) price are the only differences among suppliers of such commodities.

You don't need to be a futures trader to be seen as the supplier of a mere "commodity." You can sell computer work stations to insurance companies, but if Metropolitan Life thinks your systems are exactly the same as everyone else's, it doesn't matter whether they "really" are or not. It's the inability of the *customer* to differentiate that defines a product or service as a commodity. When there's no perceived difference, you might as well be pushing pork bellies.

There's nothing wrong with pushing pork bellies, if that's what you want to do. But in targeting Large Accounts, it's a weak position. When customers see you as supplying commodities, you have virtually no control over what happens in their accounts, and almost no chance of growing a long-term relationship. Why? Because commodity trading has very simple rules: "Buy cheap, sell dear." If your customers see what you sell as indistinguishable from what your competitors can sell, then your only bargaining chips are availability and low bid. Not a very secure position.

LEVEL 2:
"GIVING GOOD TRUCK"

On the second level of the hierarchy, you're seen as the supplier of "good" products or services—products, for example, that incorporate state-of-the-art technology, or that meet exacting technical specifications, or that are backed up by great service and support. Not just a minimally acceptable computer, but one that's extremely fast or user-friendly. Not just an overnight courier service, but one that guarantees 10 A.M. delivery. Not just a car waiting at the airport, but your name in flashing lights, showing you where it's parked.

Anything that sets you off from the competition, that gets you noticed by your customers as an innovator, can help you establish a second-level business relationship. Obviously this is an improvement. But providing "good product" is still a shaky position.

The reason is simple: competition. You can *establish* a competitive position with bells and whistles (or faster service, or other add-ons), but you can't *maintain* it. Unless you've got a patent lock on your distinctive feature or benefit—and these days, even when you do—eventually the competition not only catches up but leapfrogs over you, and you're back to selling commodity-style again, with the "distinctive" features now part of everybody's arsenal.

This happens all the time in the high-tech field. One company introduces a robo-mouse, or a graphics display, or a fiber-optic link, that immediately puts it ahead of the pack. Six months later, after everybody from Tokyo to Tucson has copied it, it has become part of the new minimum standards. And the battle goes on, cranked up another notch.

One of our clients is a large trucking firm. The president of that company joked with us a couple of years ago about the limitations of good-product positioning. With ten or twelve hungry competitors on his tail, he said, it was no longer sufficient just to "give good truck." "All the major players now give good truck. Clean, well-maintained vehicles. On-time pickup and delivery. Courteous drivers. Guarantees against breakage. All of that has become the norm now. If you want to play in this league, you have to give more and better service on top of that."

This is a good description of the advantages—and the limitations—of delivering a "better" product. Let's look now at what our friend meant by "more."

LEVEL 3:
GOING THE EXTRA MILE

At the third level of the buy-sell hierarchy, your customer sees you as providing not just good product, but good service and support in the bargain. You not only install the new, "good" phone system on time, but you provide users with a training program at no extra charge, and when the system goes down, you debug it. Quickly, professionally, with no excuses.

Going the extra mile in this manner for your customers almost always results in better business, especially in today's service-intensive economy. More and more businesses today are differentiated on the basis of how they *treat* their customers, not just what they sell them. And the leaders are the companies that do this best.

Take one of the premier success stories of the last decade: Federal Express. It leads the pack in overnight delivery not only because it gets your letter there on time—even though it "absolutely, positively" does do that. Federal Express has the lion's share of the overnight letter market because it provides such "extras" as instant computer tracking of every item, an enormous network of accessible drop-off points, and—most important—consistent, professional, and cheerful service at every step along the way, in every one of its depots.

Increasingly, the best competitors in every business are moving in the same direction as Federal Express. They have to. "Service and support" is fast replacing "features and benefits" as an entry fee for the real players. And this cranks the "minimum acceptable" level up another notch. In what business analyst Paul Hawken calls the "informative economy," suppliers who are unwilling or unable to provide such "extras" as dynamite postsale service are increasingly being squeezed out.

LEVEL 4: THE QUANTUM LEAP TO BUSINESS ISSUES

At the first three levels of business relationship, the number of players remains high. So does your customer's sensitivity to product price. Both of those things change dramatically when you make the quantum leap to the fourth level.

On the fourth level, customers perceive your company as providing not just good products and extra service, but *help in the actual running of their businesses*. When you're positioned here, you understand each account's business problems and objectives almost as well as you do your own. You generate ideas for addressing not just customers' day-to-day operational needs but their ongoing profitability concerns. You sell products and services that address those concerns. And *only* those products and services.

Example: Suppose you sell information systems to a manufacturer who is concerned about getting an inventory tangle under
control. One of your midrange systems would solve her inventory
problem quickly, efficiently, and at reasonable cost. She'd probably spring for a more expensive, top-of-the-line configuration,
though. It's loaded with features she will never use, but the sale
would double your revenue and the salesperson's commission.
Which system do you sell her?

If you're thinking long term, it's no contest. You leave the
quick-buck-and-out dodge to those companies that see their customers as easy marks, and you deliver the system that will best
meet *her* business needs. And you do it for the most pragmatic of
reasons: Over time, it will make you more money. Customers
who see you saving them money are going to seek you out beyond
this quota period: They'll want your business as much as you want
theirs.

Here's the kicker. They'll want it *even if it costs them more*. As
you become positioned toward the top of the buy-sell hierarchy,
you can charge a premium price for your products and services
because you're providing much more than mere products and
services. You're contributing something that few competitors
even think about—something your accounts will pay extra for,
without batting an eye.

This has zero to do with customers becoming your "friends."
It's a matter of enlightened self-interest. Help me lower my costs,
increase my sales, boost my profit, and you *bet* I'm going to work
with your company. And pay the freight with a smile. That's what
value-added business is all about.

LEVEL 5:
"UPPING" THE ORGANIZATION

In his 1978 business classic *Up the Organization*, onetime Avis
president Robert Townsend pointed out that, in many businesses, efficiency and profit were being hamstrung by bureau-
cratic confusion and organizational turf fights. If you've spent
more than a couple of days in a corporate structure, you know
that's true. And it gives the savvy sales professional a great opportunity. If you can help to reduce the logjams in your customers'

"internal affairs"—if you can help their ships sail smoother, day to day—they'll consider you as much an external asset as you consider them.

This happens on the top level of the buy-sell hierarchy. In the best of all business relationships with your customers, you go beyond providing them with good products, extra service, and help with their bottom-line concerns. You become an ad hoc consultant to their organizations by contributing to their efficiency *as* organizations.

Suppose one of your Large Accounts wants to shore up a faltering profit margin, and its strategy is to decentralize operations, allowing division managers greater control over their profit centers. In this scenario, any sale that breathed life into the account's profit-and-loss statement would be seen as a contribution to business issues. That's good. But even better would be a sale that improved its profit *and* facilitated the planned decentralization. Such a sale would tie in to the firm's concerns at both the market and the internal levels—for any supplier, an ideal combination.

Or take a personal example. Several years ago, during a call on a sales executive in one of our Large Accounts, it became obvious that he was preoccupied by something else. When we asked him what it was, he said he was having trouble understanding the new management by objectives program that the company had mandated. Since we were well acquainted with MBO programs, we switched the agenda of that call on the spot, spending the hour clarifying his company's new organizational directive. The meeting thus ceased to be a "sales call" and became a consulting session on upper-level concerns. Although we entered his office as salesmen, we left as partners.

It's difficult, we'll admit, to contribute consistently to your accounts' organizational issues. It's even more difficult to be *perceived* as doing so. But doing so is almost always worth the effort, because the potential differentiation from your competitors at the top of the hierarchy is tremendous. The fact is that, in spite of the account control that you can exert from the top of the hierarchy, very few companies ever get there—or even try to. Tradition and intimidation keep all but the most aggressive and innovative players from trying to do more than deliver great service. Result? There *is* room at the top. For long-term business, it's the only place to aim for.

ROOM AT THE TOP: THE ADVANTAGES

The two-directional arrows at either side of the buy-sell hierarchy indicate why this is so.

First, as you move up in the hierarchy, *competition* decreases, simply because so few companies know how to present themselves as addressing their Large Accounts' organizational and business concerns. Every business in the world pushes its products; a minuscule number are in competition to sell buyers real solutions for *their* problems. There's plenty of lip service to that effect, but little action.

Second, there's less sensitivity about *price*. If you offer not merely a good product but true added value—value added to the account's business—you're free to some degree from supply and demand curves. This doesn't necessarily mean you can charge 40 percent more than your top competitor; but you can bill, and get paid, at the high end.

Last, the importance of *features* decreases, because the contribution you're seen as making to clients' businesses outweighs the significance of anybody's bells and whistles. So you're less likely to have to "cram product" and more likely to be delivering solutions rather than promises.

As the legend above the right-hand arrow indicates, the upper-hierarchy approach to account management means providing *solutions* or improving *results*. Recall that both are defined from an account's point of view. You've got to aim for solutions to each customer's specific, bottom-line problems. The happy irony, of course, is that making such "altruistic" contributions to a customer's business is also the best way to improve your own.

"NONBUSINESS" BUSINESS SOLUTIONS

The solutions you provide for a customer's bottom-line problems don't have to be directly related to individual sales proposals. They don't even have to be related to the business that you do, or expect to do, with that customer. In some of the most sophisticated strategies we've ever seen, the selling company dramatically improved its position by providing counsel or expertise to a Large Account in a tangential or even supposedly "irrelevant" business area. Some examples:

• A midwest college was being threatened with total shutdown over seemingly unresolvable labor grievances until the company that supplied its food service loaned it a highly experienced personnel manager as an ad hoc negotiator with the college unions.

• To keep in touch with developments in retailing, Kimberly-Clark established an Executive Exchange program with the Safeway chain. Twice a year senior managers from these two companies meet to reinforce the relationship and iron out problems.

• To address the downtime threat posed by employees with substance-abuse problems, an instruments manufacturer invited executives from a customer's alcohol-troubled firm to observe the operation of its own Employee Assistance Program.

You'll notice that in none of these examples did the solution hook up directly to the seller's business. But in every one it positively affected the buy-sell *relationship*, because it addressed concerns—labor problems, marketing, productivity—that had bottom-line, upper-hierarchy implications.

COVERING ALL THE BASES

When we speak about selling at the upper level of the buy-sell hierarchy, we're emphasizing the customer's perception of your contribution. There's another sense of "upper level," however, that relates to the management hierarchy of the Large Account. In "ideal" organizational selling, these two senses reinforce each other. The best Large Account managers we know consistently present solutions to upper-level concerns, and they do so *at* the upper levels of the account's management.

This is no more than common sense. In any business, organizational and business issues are the natural bailiwick of senior management. In addition, people at that level are the only ones who can realistically commit their companies to long-term partnerships, and they're the only ones, in many cases, who can release funds. Good account management thus requires that you bring your upper-level solutions to their attention.

In recommending this, we're not saying that you should "sell at the top" and hope your senior contacts will impose your solutions on their "underlings." We don't advise anyone to ignore either lower-level issues *or* people who work at "lower" levels of an account's organization. Moving up the buy-sell hierarchy is cumulative, not exclusive. Even if your principal contact at Verve Inc. is old man Verve himself, and even if he sees you as a brilliant analyst of his firm's situation, you've still got to deliver the basic goods: the circuitry, the software, or whatever it is that you sell them. And you've got to check regularly how you're perceived by *everyone* in the customer organization who might conceivably have an impact on your sales.

Herein lies the virtue of a team approach. In positioning yourself with large organizations, you've got to cover all the bases: that is, ensure that every potential decision maker in the buying organization is contacted by the most appropriate member of your organization. But the appropriate person to call on old man Verve is unlikely to be the same person who should call on the engineering department or on the accounting whiz who's in bed with your competition. In Large Account management, we feel that, ideally, CEOs should call on CEOs, engineers on engineers, and so on. You don't have to meet this ideal. You *do* have to cover the account's concerns from the "low level" of basic product specs all the way up to the "top level" of organizational issues. For that, you need the cooperation of a team.

THE PRICE OF SECURITY: VIGILANCE

We've emphasized the importance of moving up the buy-sell hierarchy. You can also move down. Nobody does it on purpose. But it happens. The business environment today is about as predictable as a tornado, and because things are constantly changing, there's a tendency for relational positions to erode unless you work, constantly and vigorously, to sustain them.

A field rep for an industrial manufacturer told us recently how painful that discovery can be. She had fought hard for a foothold with a major account's manager of operations and had positioned herself well up the hierarchy by addressing his inventory concerns. Then, after she was "firmly established," she neglected him for several weeks—just long enough for his inventory problem to spin out of control. Because the absent are always wrong, he blamed her. When she finally showed up at his door weeks later, expecting to renew some routine orders, she had already tumbled down the hierarchy without knowing it. Poking her head into the manager's office, she inquired politely, "Ready for those orders now, Ken?"

Sure, Ken said. He had two orders. "Get out. And stay out."

We've seen it happen time and again. A strong, competitive company builds a reputation by providing solutions, by speaking to its customers' business and organization issues, by cooperating with key players and top management. But once it's perceived as a real contributor, it gets cocky, then lazy. Believing that its company's position is secure, salespeople take the customer for granted. Management starts to think of the company as a sure thing. And suddenly, without any warning, the whole thing goes to hell in a handbasket.

The only way to avoid this common problem is to remember that it's your customers, not you, who place you at a given level of the buy-sell hierarchy. They can throw you off too, if you're not looking. The moral is to look. All the time.

And to do it with the *customers'* eyes.

||7||

Seeing Through Your Customers' Eyes

To appraise any account situation, you begin by thinking with the customer's mind. It's seldom easy, and it often strikes people who sell for a living as unnatural. To action-oriented people, used to focusing fiercely on today's order log or this month's commission statement, trying to adopt a customer's perspective can sometimes seem like a mere academic exercise.

In fact, it's anything but that. From a purely practical, dollars-and-cents standpoint, you'd *better* see things as the people in your Large Accounts do, because the decisive factor in any sale is the customers' receptivity to what you're offering. That receptivity is inevitably a function of the way *their* companies, not yours, see the world.

To understand your customers' worldviews, you start by recalling the obvious: Each Large Account is a company. Like any other company (including your own), it's out there in a rough, hardball market, making its own sales, incurring its own expenses, fighting its own competitors, striving to boost its own profit line. Like your company, it's got both problems and opportunities. In some markets its share is going up, while in others it's declining. Some of its departments are running smoothly, while others are crying out for CPR. Your Large Account's managers, just like you, have their own strategic concerns and organizational priorities. And, just as in your organization, decisions are made not by totally rational "philosopher kings," but by real people—people involved in turf battles and career moves and conflicting visions of where their company is, or ought to be, moving.

All of this affects the way your Large Account's decision makers see the world, and therefore their receptivity to your company's proposals. So, if you expect to exert influence in the account, you've got to begin by assessing these factors from their perspective.

You'll do that in a second Strategy Workshop. We'll present you with a series of focused questions designed to help you analyze:

1. Your Large Account's *business situation*;
2. Its understanding of *your industry*;
3. Its view of *your competition*; and
4. Its view of *your company*.

When your team has completed this workshop, you'll understand better how this major account's players think and—just as important—you'll have identified problem or gray areas, where you really don't know how they think.

It's a long workshop. In LAMP programs, our clients spend an hour and a half on this phase of situation appraisal. We recommend that you spend at least an hour. So open your notebook, put the heading "Situation Appraisal" at the top of a blank page, and write answers to the following questions *from your targeted account's point of view.*

If you don't know an answer, or if you think that two or more people in the account would have different answers, write *that* down. And plan to make whatever calls are necessary to find out the answers, directly, from the account. The more you involve your customer in account planning, the less guesswork you'll have to contend with. Ideally, people from the targeted Large Account should be present as you work through this material. If that's not possible, you should still actively solicit their comments on this workshop, so your view of their view is based on solid information.

STRATEGY WORKSHOP 2:
SITUATION APPRAISAL/CUSTOMER'S VIEW

Step 1. Analyze the customer's business situation.

First, review your account's current business performance. In your notebook under the subheading "Business Situation," write down brief notes—we suggest short phrases or one-line observations—to help you clarify the following:

• *Profit and loss performance*. What were the account's sales and profit figures for the past year? For the past three? Is there an upward or downward trend discernible in these figures, or has the company's performance been flat? Look at these figures not just in terms of the entire company's performance but in terms of your selected portion of the account. Most annual reports break down P&L figures at least to the division level; you want a financial snapshot of your "field of play."

• *Competition*. What is your account's competitive position? Who are *its* major competitors? What is its market share? In the past two or three years, has that share grown or fallen? What major pressures are being brought against it now, either by traditional rivals or by new players in the market?

• *Market forces*. What economic trends are affecting the account's industry as a whole? In setting strategy, you'll want to position yourself one way with a company that's riding an industry growth curve and quite another way for an industry in a mature or shakeout phase. Do the account's microtrends reflect, or run against, the macroforces? Are a bull market and a rising economy working in the customer's favor? Or are recessionary forces affecting the firm's ability to compete effectively?

If you were selling to the oil or automotive industries, for example, you'd want to be aware of oil price trends before you even began to think about setting sales strategy. To be ignorant of such basic information might lead you to adopt strategic positions that were appropriate in 1989 but hopelessly out of date two years later.

• *Organization*. To have influence in a Large Account, you must be aware of, and in sync with, who's on top organizationally. So look at the account's internal structure. What's the internal balance among marketing, production, and finance people? Marketers pursue sales revenue and market share. Production people favor proposals that reduce costs and streamline schedules. Finance wants return on investment and steady profit. The mix of these three can dramatically affect an account's purchasing policy.

Look also at the stability, or instability, of the organization. Is it centralizing, decentralizing, or in some other way changing its management structure? *Don't minimize internal changes.* They're always relevant to the way a business makes decisions. After the decentralization of AT&T, for example, it took our company several arduous months to figure out the new mix of key players and authority levels. Trying to do serious business with this Large Account without figuring that out, however, would have been like throwing darts in the dark.

• *Politics.* What about governmental pressures? What regulatory controls is the firm facing? Is it part of a heavily controlled or loosely controlled industry? What legislative changes on the horizon might impact, positively or negatively, the way it does business? If you were selling anything to a major airline in the late 1970s, for example, you had to reconsider your sales strategy totally when the Reagan administration's deregulation measures began to "loosen up" the skies. Within a matter of months, the air routes that American and Delta and United had run for years suddenly came up for "reassignment." The impact on the carriers' business was a scramble for niches, but the impact on those who sold to the airlines was no less profound: Suddenly every airline account was a different animal.

Look, too, for political "events," domestic or international, that could affect the way your Large Account runs its affairs. Iraq's 1990 invasion of Kuwait provides only the most obvious and dramatic example: The ripples from that faraway event have changed the way nearly everyone is doing business.

• *Other facts.* What other facts, trends, or even possibilities are currently having an impact on this Large Account? Write down anything you think *it* might consider important. The poor health of a key executive, the introduction of a new technology, a reduction in its end users' disposable income—anything that might *in any way* affect its business.

Caution: *Don't* look just for those elements of the situation

that relate to *your* business. Your Large Account isn't in business
to serve you. Note concerns that, for whatever reason, matter to
this Large Account.

Step 2. The customer's view of your industry.

Next, look at how the account sees your industry—or, more
precisely, your industry's place in *its* business.

• *General practice*. What is this account's overall purchasing
practice or "philosophy" regarding your industry? Does it go
consistently with the lowest bid? Spread its purchases among
three or four suppliers on a preferred vendor list? Or demonstrate loyalty to proven suppliers in spite of fluctuations in price
or value? Based on what it's bought from you in the past two or
three years, is it a good candidate for value-added selling, or is
low cost the firm's primary consideration?

• *Selection criteria*. What criteria does the account use when
buying? How much flexibility is built into its specification requirements? What relative importance does it assign to product
specs, price, availability, and such "extra" features as delivery
time, service capability, and support? Be sure to note variations
that might exist between different product or service areas, and
between the account's divisions or business units. You want to
isolate the criteria that are used to decide between you and your
competitors in your designated field of play.

• *Key players*. Who makes or influences buying decisions? In
sales to Large Accounts, several people are typically involved in
selecting vendors. Ideally, you should list here *all* the people who
can impact on your business with this Large Account, from internal users of your products to outside consultants.

Look especially for people we call Economic Buyers. The
Economic Buyer is the person who, on an individual decision to
buy, gives (or withholds) final approval. Exercising ultimate economic control, he or she can find money that doesn't exist in the
established budget and can also veto a sale for "lack of funds." No
company has a single individual who plays this role for all sales.
However, in most Large Accounts, there are a number of influen-
tial senior managers who consistently exert some degree of con-

trol over large purchases, and these people's perceptions of your company can be critical factors in developing—or hurting—a relationship.

• *Purchase trends.* Have there been recent changes in the pattern of this account's purchasing? Some of our clients, in thinking about this, find that the introduction of Star Trek technology is changing the solutions their Large Accounts are looking for. Others say that the deregulation impetus of the Reagan-Bush era has made their customers more open to innovation. Still others perceive no changes; they see the purchasing trend as steady rather than directional.

Pay special attention to two trends: One, the volume of the account's purchasing in your *industry.* Is it rising, falling, or holding steady? Two, the percentage of this volume that the account sends your company. What's your current share in your field of play? And is that share rising, falling, or holding steady?

• *Customer's attitude.* Finally, what is the Large Account's general attitude toward doing business with your industry? Does it consider it a necessary evil? Essential to its success? Or does it see reliance on your industry as part of a mutually beneficial partnership? Admittedly, this is subjective. But that doesn't mean it's invalid. Your customer's gut feelings about your industry *directly* affect his or her receptivity to your products and services. Determining how people in the Large Account feel about your business is therefore a hard-nosed, pragmatic endeavor.

Step 3. The customer's view of your competition.

You are not the best judge of your competition. Your customer is. Therefore, you're now going to get a fix on how this Large Account views the single greatest threat to your success—your major competitor for its business. This is even more subjective than what you've done so far—probably too subjective for you or your account team to pull off alone. For this reason, we underline the advice that we gave at the beginning of the workshop: To determine how they feel, *ask people in your Large Account directly.*

In this and the next step of the workshop, you'll be "rating" your major competitor and then yourself on a simple 1 to 10 scale. This isn't the higher math or a *Psychology Today* quiz. Use the scale as our corporate clients do: not to score points or to "quantify" your situation but to get an indication of how your company's doing, how the competition's doing, and how the two of you stack up in the Large Account's eyes.

With your notebook lying flat, divide a left-hand page into three columns. At the top of the far-left column, write the heading "How Customer Sees." Head the center column "Competition" and the right-hand column "Our Company." In the left-hand column, copy down the following seven categories of assessment:

- Level of business relationship
- Understanding of customer's business situation
- Product fit to customer's needs
- Positioning in customer's organization
- Product/service reputation
- Prices
- Helpfulness to customer

Then rate how your customer views your major competitor with regard to each of these categories, using a 1 if the customer's view is extremely negative and a 10 if it's the best it can be.

For example, suppose your customer believes your competitor has little or no understanding of his or her business situation: The competitor would receive a 1 or 2 on this item. If the competitor's prices are about average for the market, you'd rate them a 5 or a 6. If the customer believes the competitor's products fit his or her needs very well, the competitor might get a 9 or 10 there.

Write down the individual ratings in your notebook. Then total them.

Step 4. Customer's view of your company.

Now work through the assessment process again, this time rating how *your* company is doing in the customer's eyes. Again, if you're not sure how you're perceived by the customer, *ask*.

When you're done rating both yourself and your competitor, you'll have a chart that looks something like this:

How Customer Sees	Competition	Our Company
Level of business relationship	7	9
Understanding of customer's business situation	7	8
Product fit to customer's need	9	5
Positioning in customer's organization	7	8
Product/service reputation	8	8
Prices	4	5
Helpfulness to customer	7	9
TOTAL	49	52

Step 5. Comparative analysis.

Now take a look at the two ratings together. Resist the temptation to "keep score." You've organized your account information in this chart to give you a quick-and-dirty view of what's going on, not to "prove" that you're acing out the competition, or that it's got you on the run. In the example we've given here, comparing the competition's total of 49 with your company's total of 52 doesn't say anything as solid as "We're edging them out with this account"—the difference isn't statistically that significant. Unless the difference between the two totals is quite large (say, 20 points), you should be wary of concluding "from the numbers" that either you or your competitor is better positioned.

Instead of drawing hasty conclusions from the totals, you

should look at the individual *line items*. Then try to identify the *three* most important facts about your account's appraisal of the situation. In our example, these might be the significant gap between "them" and "us" with regard to product fit (9 to 5), or the fact that the account sees little difference between you and the competition in terms of price (5 to 4). In addition, ask yourself the following questions, designed to qualify the quantified comparison:

• What are our competitor's chief *advantages*, as perceived by this customer?

• What does this customer *need*, now or in the future, that cannot be easily obtained from the competition?

• What would it take for the customer to buy from us what he or she now buys from the competition?

• In what areas of the customer's organization is such a change of purchasing policy likely to happen?

• In order for it to happen, must the policy be changed at a higher level of the organization than the one where we're currently positioned?

RECONSIDERING THE RELATIONSHIP: HOW ARE WE DOING? (AGAIN)

The final question here relates, both organizationally and conceptually, to the buy-sell relational hierarchy. It's appropriate to close this chapter on your customer's view by returning to the hierarchy, because nothing in an account's appraisal of a situation has more impact on your sales potential than *its* view of your business relationship.

We found dramatic evidence of this fact in a recent workshop. Our client was a regional division of AT&T, and the division's targeted account was a university. In terms of product capability, the AT&T people could offer an extremely good fit to the university's needs, yet they were having serious problems in expanding their penetration of this Large Account beyond a rather limited client commitment to long-line service. "Somehow," one account team member told us, "they just don't seem to see how much *more* helpful we could be to them, if they'd let us try."

Fortunately, the AT&T account team, following our advice,

had invited the university's telecommunications chief to be a participant in the LAMP session. At one point in the "Customer's View" section of the analysis, one team member turned to the guest and articulated his frustration by blurting out "Just how do you see us, anyway?"

The frank answer surprised everybody but the university manager himself. "We've been buying from regional networks for fifty years," he said. "We see you as the new kid on the block."

An "objective" observer might say that seeing the largest telecommunications company in the world as a "kid" was a little ridiculous. But it made perfect sense to the manager, and to the AT&T account team, it was a revelation. It made them recognize, in a way that no amount of market research could have made them recognize, that the hundred-year-old Ma Bell reputation meant next to nothing on this campus and that they would have to plan their strategy, therefore, "around" it.

In the words of the participant who'd asked the question, "When I heard that, it was like the first cup of coffee in the morning. For the first time, I stopped thinking *about* the account and started thinking about the world as *they* saw it."

Which is the essential way to see it, if you want their business.

|8|

Using
Your Own Eyes

Having completed an involved analysis of how your customer sees you, you're now going to perform a relatively simple analysis of how you and your team see this same customer. The brevity of this second analysis doesn't mean we consider your perspective unimportant. But we've found that many account management teams concentrate almost exclusively on their own perspective—which leads, inevitably, to tunnel vision. That's why we take the Large Account's view first and then check it against what you know and feel.

Note that the "feel" is just as important as the "know." Our experience has shown time and again that you should never discount your gut feelings about an account. Therefore, in this workshop, you'll assess your chosen Large Account not just in terms of hard data like sales figures but also in terms of values and attitudes. To do so, you'll use a numerical rating scale that's similar to the one you just used to measure your customer's perceptions. It's not exactly the same scale, because your interests aren't identical with those of your customers. But it will generate the same kind of rough guide, to provide a check on the assessments you've just done.

STRATEGY WORKSHOP 3:
SITUATION APPRAISAL/OUR VIEW

Step 1. Evaluate the account.

On a left-hand page of your notebook, you've rated your customer's view of your company and of your competition. On the right-hand, facing page, copy down the following seven assessment categories, leaving space next to each one for a numerical rating:

Its sales trend (2–3 years out)   ____

Its growth vs. our strengths   ____

How coachable its people are   ____

How much we enjoy working with the account   ____

Showcase/referral source for us   ____

Recent trend of orders   ____

How much it helps us   ____

Now rate this Large Account numerically, on a 1 to 10 scale, based on how it stacks up in each category. Here are some guidelines to help you:

Sales trend. We mean *the customer's* sales trend—how well the Large Account is doing in its own market. You want to know this up front because it's an indicator of the firm's receptivity to future business with you. If its sales are declining, give the firm a 1. If they're going through the roof—or if it looks like they might in the near future—give them a 9 or a 10.

Growth/strength. Once you've determined how quickly (or slowly) the customer's business is growing, you want to find out whether its growth pattern gives *your* company a sales advantage. No matter how fast the personal computer market is growing, for example, it presents only a limited opportunity to a software company whose product line is the same as every other software company's. You need to determine how well your company's specific capabilities play (or can play) into the customer's areas of growth. If all your competitors can meet its growth needs just as well as you can, its rating should be a 1 or a 2; if you're the sole source, give it a 10.

"Coachability." Aside from what you can actually sell this customer, are its people interested in what you have to say? Can you serve as a "coach" to them, either with regard to your shared concerns or with regard to business or organizational issues? Do they trust you well enough to listen to your advice, or is your association based on "just business"? The ratings here might run from a 1 for an antagonistic customer, through 5 or 6 for one who listens to what you say, to 10 for one who actively seeks your advice.

Enjoy working with the account. When you feel great about working with an account, it's a signal you've established a solid relationship that is seen by both parties as beneficial. If you hate making calls on the account, by definition you don't have such a relationship; you're probably perceived as a commodity. To get a handle on where you are in the relational hierarchy, assess how much you dislike (1 to 2) or really enjoy (9 to 10) doing business with this Large Account.

Showcase/referral source. One indicator of a business relationship's health is the readiness of a customer to let you use him or her as an example of how well you deliver. Would you take a new prospect into this customer's plant or offices to show off your partnership? If you can't get a good reference from this account— or if you aren't willing to ask for one—you need to reexamine the relationship. A 1 account is one you'd rather not have your other customers see; a 10 account is the best place to take prospects.

Order trend. Has the firm been buying more from you lately, or less? What's your market share with this account? How does it compare to your major competitor's share? And how does it tie in, over the past two or three years, with the customer's growth profile? If the firm is growing but your orders aren't, where's the problem? If its orders are declining, the account's a 1; if they're skyrocketing, it's a 9 or a 10.

Helpfulness. We've stressed that you've got to help your customers, not only by providing them with the goods they need but also by addressing their business and organizational needs. They've got to help you too. How well does this customer do that? Do the contacts not only accept your coaching, but coach your people in return? Do they understand how your business works, and do they want a mutually supportive association? Or is working with them all take and no give? A company that causes you lots of problems is a 1; if its people go out of their way to support you, rate the firm a 10.

Once you've finished this rating exercise, add up the individual ratings for a total. Your rating chart should now look something like this:

Our View of (Large Account)

Its sales trend (2–3 years out)	7
Its growth vs. our strength	8
How coachable its people are	8
How much we enjoy working with the account	9
Showcase/referral source	6
Trend of orders	8
How much it helps us	5
TOTAL	51

Step 2. Compare the customer's view with yours.

Now turn back to the numerical rating you constructed in the previous workshop, and compare your customer's view of you with your view of the customer.

Take both assessments seriously. Don't assume that they're "right" and you're "wrong"—or vice versa. As critical as the account appraisal is, it's not gospel. Taking a "good" assessment as blanket approval, or a "bad" one as an invitation to pull out, can be just as ill advised as insisting, as one of our corporate clients jokes, that "Our service isn't as bad as they think." The point is to bring useful information—including contrasting views—to the surface, not to play Jeopardy with your external assets.

Compare individual line items as well as totals. Suppose, as in the example, you score the customer's view of you at 52 and your view of the customer at 51. Does that mean you've got no problems? Not necessarily. The true value of this exercise lies in the line items: in comparing, for example, how well you help the account versus how well it helps you. Or how the two of you see your products fitting, or not fitting, with the customer's business. You can get exactly the same macrototals on these roughly equivalent scales, but if there are serious microdiscrepancies, you'll have to address them when you're setting strategy.

Finally, *extrapolate* from the raw scores. That is, discuss honestly as a team what it means to be 20 points out of whack with this customer. Up *or* down. For example, if the company's score for you is a 29 and yours for the company is a 48, it is probably not as eager as you are to build the relationship into the future. On the other hand, if those scores are reversed, you may not be pursuing the firm's business as aggressively as you should be. The goal of this rating exercise, once again, is not to "score" you against other players in the field. It's to check your thinking about your relationship and your current position.

Step 3. Review your Charter Statement.

Now use the information you've pulled together in this workshop to review and, if necessary, revise your Charter Statement.

In that statement, you defined three things: the field of play that you sell to, what you sell, and the added value that you bring to the Large Account's business. In light of the information you've uncovered in the last two workshops, how realistic is that definition? Have you clearly identified the segment of the Large Account with which you have been forging a relationship? Is it as clear to the company as it is to you what products and services you can deliver? Most important of all, does the customer clearly perceive the contribution that your company makes to his or her business and organizational issues? To the bottom line?

If the answers to any of these questions are negative or unclear, reassess your Charter Statement. Write down the relevant information you've uncovered and what's still missing. As a team discuss where to get the missing pieces, who should get them, and when.

Once you've revised and polished the Charter Statement, it will be time to pull together everything you've done so far, in another appraisal of the account situation. That's the project, and the process, of the next chapter.

9

Putting It All Together

So far your situation appraisal has consisted of gathering data. A lot of it. We've thrown dozens of questions at you, designed to bring to the surface information about your account and to show you where you're missing information. Now you're going to *distill* from this mass of information the five elements that are most critical in understanding your position: Strengths, Opportunities, Trends, Key Players, and Vulnerability. After we define each one, you'll identify them in your targeted Large Account. By the end of this chapter, you'll have organized your account data into a document called a Situation Appraisal Summary. This summary will contain, on a single page, the most significant, and usable, data that you need for setting Large Account strategy.

STRENGTHS: THE IMPORTANCE OF UNIQUENESS

One company's strength is another's weakness. That obvious fact leads us to define Strengths comparatively, in terms of what economists call competitive advantage. We say that a true Strength gives you an edge. It's not just an area in which you're "good," but one in which you're *different* from the competition.

When Johnson Wax president Samuel Johnson was a product manager under his father, Sam Senior, he came up with an idea for an insecticide. The elder man asked him how it was different from what was already out there. The son had to admit that its features were shared by many other insecticides, and so he trooped back to the research lab until he came up with a product that *was* different—a water-based aerosol that didn't smell like an insecticide. The product soon led the field in domestic bug sprays. Plenty of other sprays worked just as well. But only Raid offered the *unique* Strength of a flowery smell.

A second example. When Kimberly-Clark first entered the disposable diaper market, it did so with a product called Kimbies. Kimbies were attractively packaged, competitive in price, and kept the baby dry; but the entrenched leader, Procter & Gamble's Pampers, did all this too. Result: no differentiation. Then Kimberly-Clark dropped its We're-just-as-good-as approach, added leg elastic to their design, and renamed their product Huggies. With the new, unique Strength, sales took off.

In our second book, *Conceptual Selling*, we argued that the uniqueness of the solutions you offer a customer typically impact his or her buying decision more profoundly than the "objective" features and benefits of a product or service. Still true. The perfect Strength is something only you can offer. Next best is what we've called a "relatively unique" Strength—a Strength that is closer to being "one of a kind" than anything your competition can deliver. The one "strength" that is *not* a Strength is the me-too solution—the capability, no matter how good, that everyone shares. As we stressed in chapter 6, there's no positioning advantage in meeting minimum specs.

FINDING THE OPPORTUNITY YOU CAN'T KNOCK

Our definition of strategic Opportunities, like our definition of strategic Strengths, is less diffuse than the usual definition. To many companies, *any* opening in a market or account is an "opportunity" not to be ignored. Endearing optimism, but poor strategy. We've encountered hundreds of situations where companies, eager to respond to every request for proposal, spread themselves so thin that, as Woody Guthrie might have put it, "even a politician could see through them." The fact is, you *lose* business by running to the door every time somebody knocks.

So in defining Opportunity, we're more selective. We say concentrate on Opportunities with true *strategic* potential. In Large Account management, this means Opportunities with *at least* a one-year impact.

While Strengths exist in your organization, Opportunities exist "out there," in the account or the market at large. The fact that your marketing department has just put together a "revolutionary" new configuration for fiber-optics transmission may (or may not) be a Strength. It's certainly not an Opportunity. A current or potential customer's *need* for such a configuration over the next five years—*that's* a strategic Opportunity.

We know a U.S. manufacturer who has been selling engine assemblies to a Finnish firm for twenty years. For even longer than that, the Finns have had close business ties with the Soviets. For years the American company tried to get federal government licenses to allow the Finns to transship its assemblies to Soviet factories, and for years the company had been turned down. Then, in November of 1989, the Berlin Wall started to crumble, signaling a dramatic shift in possibilities. Within months the State and Commerce departments had begun to loosen their restrictions, providing an extraordinary opening for the American manufacturer in a market that had been closed to it before. Its solid products, and its solid positioning with the Finns, were Strengths; the unexpected opening was a strategic Opportunity.

Even if you narrow the door knockers down to the one year or more Opportunities, you'll still have a pretty wide field. We suggest that, in doing LAMP analysis, you focus on the ones that are so good in terms of potential returns that it would make you uncomfortable to ignore or postpone them. As we'll demonstrate in chapters 12 and 13, focusing on one Opportunity always means sacrificing another. The Opportunities that you address in a LAMP strategy are the ones that say "Act now, or live to regret it."

TRENDS: UP, DOWN, AND "CONSTANT"

After Strengths and Opportunities, the third critical element in setting strategy is Trends. These can relate to developments in your business, in your customer's business, in the business environment as a whole—or all three. The defining characteristic of a strategic Trend is that, wherever you find it, it reflects *change* over time.

The time element is essential. In the first Beatles' film, *A Hard Day's Night*, a pop star's nervous agent considers dropping her contract in response to one negative comment on her performance. "It might be a trend," he mutters. That's trend-spotting by paranoia—the kind of knee-jerk situation appraisal that leads to copy-cat and tail-chasing "strategies." To avoid joining the Nervous Nelly school of business forecasting, look for Trends that have been developing for a year or more. Some examples:

- Increased foreign competition.
- A greater awareness of environmental issues.
- Rising health consciousness among consumers.
- Increased speed of communications.
- Globalization of markets.
- Growth in liability lawsuits.
- Decrease in customer "loyalty."

To these widespread economic Trends, you can add examples of changes that are peculiar to your industry and markets and even to your company and customer base.

Look, in particular, for direction. A Trend might move up, down, or overseas, but it's unlikely it will ever be "constant." Few "flat-growth" profiles, for example, are truly flat—for the simple reason that the environment is not static. Say a customer has been a reliable revenue stream for the past five years—$250,000 in orders a year, every year. That may look like flat growth, but if inflation has been eating away at the value of that revenue, and if the market you're selling to is expanding, then your "steady-state" customer isn't flat at all. In the environment you both inhabit, the real Trend of his or her business is down.

One further caveat. If in spotting Opportunities you want to be optimistic, in spotting Trends a little pessimism is in order. Our advice is to look for *negative* Trends as fervently as you look for positive ones. If a globalizing market, or the introduction of a competitive technology, or the surge in oil prices, seems like a threat rather than an Opportunity for your business, don't deny it. Threats can often be turned into Opportunities—but only if you see them for what they are.

KEY PLAYERS: THE BIG THREE

In managing a Large Account, you may deal with ten, twenty, or one hundred individuals who can, positively or negatively, affect your business relationship. We don't advise you to ignore any of these people, and in fact our oldest program, Strategic Selling, is specifically designed to help salespeople identify *all* the decision makers in individual sales.

In LAMP, we move beyond the individual sale to focus on those few individuals who, consistently and predictably over time, are most likely to affect your influence in the account. We call these individuals Key Players. They fall into three basic categories.

Sponsor.

The sponsor of a television program underwrites and endorses its activities. In LAMP analysis people whom we call Sponsors perform a similar function for your account team. Sponsors must fulfill two requirements:

First, they must exercise authority or influence over that portion of the Large Account that you've chosen as your field of play. Sponsors don't have complete control of the decision-making process (nobody does), but their voices carry weight in the account. Therefore, what they say can have an impact on how you're perceived in your chosen field of play.

Second, they must support your "tenancy" in the account. Sponsors see their *own self-interest* served by the development of a relationship between their firm and yours. Maybe they have been involved in a successful partnership with you in the past and increased their internal credibility as a result. Maybe they see the solutions that your company can offer as improving the productivity of their department. If a manufacturing manager, for example, was experiencing a quality control problem and he saw your firm as the source of ongoing solutions, then he could very likely become a Sponsor. By definition Sponsors want you in there—not just for a given proposal, but over the long term.

Strategic Coach.

A football coach gives advice and counsel to the players. He doesn't run the plays himself, but he helps to make them happen. Coaches in a buy-sell relationship do the same. They provide reliable and usable information on how you can position yourself more effectively.

In *Strategic Selling*, we speak of Coaches for individual sales proposals. Strategic Coaches play a different, wider role; their impact on your work is accountwide. To have such an impact, they must meet three criteria:

1. Strategic Coaches must have major influence, and often actual authority, in the Large Account *beyond* your chosen field of play. Good Strategic Coaches have high credibility with upper management and are respected at all levels of the company's hierarchy.

2. They must support your efforts in the account. For whatever reason, they also want you in there, over the long term.

3. Strategic Coaches, because of their upper-management position, must provide solid information on how the entire Large Account operates and makes decisions. They are able, and willing, to coach you not just on single sales efforts but on improving your *position* in the account.

There are obvious similarities between a Sponsor and a Coach, and it's not uncommon for one person to be both. A senior manager who can explain the workings of her organization *and* who wants a long-term relationship with your company might easily fill both sponsoring roles. But this doesn't mean that all Sponsors are (or can become) Strategic Coaches. A Strategic

Coach understands the entire account, not just his or her immediate area of authority. The manufacturing manager with the quality control problem, for example, probably would not make a good Strategic Coach: His area of operations is too narrow. But the general manager of his division, or the vice president in charge of manufacturing—each would be suitable as a Strategic Coach.

If you don't have a Strategic Coach in place, make developing one a priority. In the effective management of account information, nothing is more useful than a top-level insider who knows how you're perceived, accountwide. Recently, for example, Hewlett-Packard reassessed its strategic approach to Boeing Aircraft. Among the most valued members of its "extended account team" was a divisional general manager from Boeing itself. HP had spent years developing a relationship with this man; the coaching insights he was able to offer in return were something that no amount of research or consulting time could buy.

Antisponsor.

Like a Sponsor and a Strategic Coach, an Antisponsor is credible to the buying organization. He or she may exert influence on how the account makes buying decisions. And that's the danger, because the Antisponsor, by definition, wants you *out*. Whatever else he or she may do in the account, as far as you're concerned the Antisponsor's role is to negate your efforts to improve your position.

Sometimes the Antisponsor's opposition is based on a difference in business philosophy. In the manufacturing firm that we've mentioned, there might be a financial vice president who seeks to block your proposals on the simple grounds that your company is not the lowest bidder. That person would be an obvious Antisponsor.

In other cases a key player may want you out over something as ostensibly "trivial" as turf rivalry. We've seen countless relationships run into trouble because an Antisponsor was categorically opposed to *everything* that a Strategic Coach or Sponsor wanted to accomplish. In other cases, Antisponsors see their self-interest being served by supporting your competition's entrenched position. Or they may be outside consultants who see your attempt to build a relationship with the Large Account as a threat to their authority. The one constant: They are opposed to your presence.

Sponsors and Coaches are relatively easy to find, because usually they want to be found. Not so with Antisponsors. They can be extremely difficult to ferret out. But invisibility doesn't mean they're not there. Almost without exception, having a Sponsor means you *also* have an Antisponsor: The one generates the other. Therefore, developing an effective account strategy always includes identifying these negative Key Players and then exploring ways to "negate their negation." Antisponsors can be converted to understanding that their self-interest does *not* run counter to yours. They can be neutralized by the effective use of Sponsors and Strategic Coaches. The one thing they *cannot* be is ignored.

VULNERABILITY: YOUR ACHILLES' HEEL

The final element to identify before setting strategy is the one that many inexperienced "strategists" focus on first. Or, even worse, focus on exclusively. We can't explain why this happens, but it's true: When we advise our clients to locate their Strengths and Opportunities, the first thing many of them say is "What about weaknesses?"

Vulnerabilities are, literally speaking, places where you can be wounded. Yes, you need to identify weaknesses. But so many companies waste time trying to guard themselves against scratches that, on this score, we reverse the conventional wisdom. We say focus your efforts on playing from Strengths, and focus your Strengths on long-term Opportunities. When it comes to donning armor against your competition, concentrate on the *one* significant weakness that, if left unprotected, could cripple your strategy. Look for what a friend of ours calls the deal killer or what the more classically minded might call an Achilles' heel.

No doubt about it. Unidentified Achilles' heels *can* do you in. In the most recent campaign of the cola wars, for example, the capture of a major fast-food client turned on the inability of one major cola player to service the franchises it sold to. It had a multimillion-dollar account in its pocket and then lost it because it failed to fix that problem.

Or take a positive example from our own business. In discussions with a large accounting firm, we discovered that although its interest in our programs was very strong, its people didn't feel they could implement them effectively unless we programmed our workshop exercises for computer. We had no facilities for doing that, but it became obvious, as the discussions proceeded, that unless we found a way to do it, we'd lose the account. So we did it: By involving a software company in the programming, we were able to develop a three-way joint venture that eliminated the Vulnerability that would have killed us. Because it was the only way to get this extremely valuable piece of business, it was worth the effort.

Few weaknesses, however, are such clear-cut deal killers. Those few you have to identify and neutralize. But you cannot build a strategy that really works by adopting what is essentially a defensive posture. If Achilles had done that, he'd have never left home.

STRATEGY WORKSHOP 4:
SITUATION APPRAISAL SUMMARY

In this workshop you'll identify the five elements we've just discussed. The physical outcome will be a one-page distillation of data that we call a Situation Appraisal Summary. We provide a blank form of that document here. Copy the headings and numbers into your notebook. You and your team will need about an hour to distill the needed data.

Step 1. Strengths.

A sound strategy capitalizes on Strengths by focusing them on Opportunities. In the situation appraisal work you've been doing, you've uncovered numerous Strengths. Eventually every one of them may become part of a Large Account strategy. For your current strategy and your current field of play, however,

SITUATION APPRAISAL SUMMARY

Strengths

1. _____
2. _____
3. _____

Opportunities

1. _____
2. _____
3. _____
4. _____

Trends

1. _____
2. _____
3. _____

Key Players

1. _____
2. _____
3. _____

Vulnerability

1. _____

you should identify the *three* greatest Strengths you can bring to bear on the Opportunities in this account. List those three winners now.

In selecting these three major Strengths, remember that you're looking internally. By definition Strengths exist in your organization, your people, your product line. But remember too that to be real Strengths, they have to connect *uniquely* to the customer, in a way your competitors' Strengths cannot. Therefore, ask yourself:

- Can this Strength be offered *only* by us—or at least *better* by us than by anybody else?
- What's the specific *contribution* that this Strength can bring to the Large Account's business? In other words, why should *the customer* care that we're uniquely strong here?

Step 2. Opportunities.

Just like Henry Ford with his Model T, you want to focus on your best Opportunities. We give you a little more latitude than he gave himself. Rather than ask you to concentrate all your resources on one history-making Opportunity, we say narrow the field of best bets down to *four.*

Again, your investigation of the account up to this point may have surfaced more than four Opportunities. But you can't tackle all of them at once. So start with the four best, and ask yourself:

- Does this Opportunity exist in the *account* rather than in our organization? Your terrific product is not an Opportunity; your customer's interest in it or need for it may be.
- Will concentrating on this Opportunity bring us good returns for at least a year or more? If not, is the expected return from a shorter time span *so* good that it justifies pursuing this Opportunity at the expense of others?
- Are there Opportunities that we'd just as soon (or rather) address than this one? If so, it's not one of the four. Your four best are the ones you've *got* to tackle.

Step 3. Trends.

Now, out of the Trends you've surfaced, identify those that are most significant for the way you do business with this Large Account. Pick *three* and write them down. Recall that Trends can exist in your business, in the customer's, or in the market at large. When you've selected them, check their significance by asking:

• Is this an enduring Trend? Has it been developing for at least a year, and is it likely to continue, for at least another, in the same direction? Blips or dips on a time line don't count.

• Because strategy capitalizes on Strengths, can you tie in this Trend to one of your three greatest Strengths? If you or your team is having trouble deciding which of five Trends are most significant, ask which ones you're best positioned to capitalize on. A "megatrend" *you* can't use is not significant.

• Similarly, because strategy focuses on Opportunities, can you link this Trend to one of your four best? If not, identifying it as a Trend may be valid but irrelevant.

Step 4. Key Players.

Out of the many people you deal with in your targeted Large Account, identify those who are most important in your field of play. Look for the three types of Key Player we've defined: Sponsor, Strategic Coach, and Antisponsor.

You may not be able, at this point, to identify one of each type. Fine. Write down the names of whichever individuals your team considers most important in your relationship with this account. However they break down in terms of the "Big Three," they'll still tell you something about your position in the account and about what kinds of relationships you need to develop to improve that position.

A few guidelines. First, if you don't have a Sponsor, consider which of the people you've identified might be turned into one. Who is most receptive to your presence at this time? Could that same person, or someone else, become a Strategic Coach?

Second, don't be fooled into believing that you don't have an Antisponsor in this account. The chances are virtually nil that *someone* in the account organization isn't antagonistic to, suspicious of, or in some other way resistant to your influence. Missing information imperils strategy, so, if you can't identify even one Antisponsor at this point, mark that up as a danger sign. Go to the people in the Large Account who are most receptive and ask, "Who wants us out?"

Third, don't settle for identifying fewer than three or four players who can in some manner (positive or negative) affect your strategy. If they don't jump out at you now, you've got to find or develop them. The most tenuous position we know is to base a strategy on a single Key Player. If that person proves unreliable, is transferred, or dies, then your "strategy" immediately becomes a house of cards.

Step 5. Vulnerability.

Now write down your single, most glaring Vulnerability. Like all businesses, you probably have more than one weakness. Your decision-making process is too slow, or you've overextended yourself in a test market, or there's a muddled liaison between your branch and divisional managers, or you don't have a clear Sponsor in the account. Any or all of these weaknesses could hurt you. We're asking you to select the *single* one that, if left untended, could do you in. If you feel that more than one could do you in, pick the one that would do the job quickest.

If you find that there's real disagreement on this point, either you haven't taken the "killer" definition seriously, and you're hunting for *any* weakness, however minor; or you really do have more than one soft spot where letting things go could imperil your position. If you *must* pay attention to two, by all means do so. But more than two "heels" become suspect.

In identifying major weaknesses, there's never a single "right" answer. There doesn't need to be. Because LAMP analysis is dynamic, eventually you'll get to address all your areas of vulnerability. Start now by making an informed guess at what hurts (or could hurt) the most.

Step 6. Check and revise.

You've now listed fourteen separate items: three Strengths, four Opportunities, three Trends, three Key Players, and one Vulnerability. Your Situation Appraisal Summary should now resemble the filled-in model we give on page 96. Next, spend a minute or so on each item, justifying your selections. On the summary form, write one-line or short-phrase explanations of each choice. "Its Mexican plant is a good Opportunity because it's an untapped multimillion-dollar market." "Rich Onoro is an Antisponsor because he's married to our competitor's CEO." "We're vulnerable in pushing the Favax transformer because we're still in midrange with quality control testing." If you can't come up with a good, short justification for each choice, it may not be as significant as you think. Rethink and revise where needed.

ANOTHER "FINAL" DRAFT: WHERE YOU ARE NOW

The summary you've constructed in this workshop gives you a concise, reasonably detailed view of where you stand *now* with regard to one field of play in one Large Account. You'll be using it for the balance of the LAMP program to set strategies, establish realistic sales Goals and Objectives, and define the various elements of an Account Plan.

Just like the Charter Statement you wrote in chapter 5, however, this Situation Appraisal Summary is also tentative. It represents your best thinking about the account today. But due to the dynamic nature of organizations—yours and your customer's—the summary *can't* be complete. You'll revise and update it as you proceed.

So don't worry if it's unclear in some particulars, or if pieces of the picture seem missing. You've just laid the foundation for a strategy, by describing your Large Account reality in the present. Now you'll look toward the future, and start building.

SITUATION APPRAISAL SUMMARY

Strengths

1. Best testing equipment on market
2. Engineering flexibility: we can customize products quickly
3. Detailed knowledge of their quality problem

Opportunities

1. Their interest in robotics
2. Opening of their new plant in Mexico
3. Their quality control program needs fixing
4. They've just gotten large subassembly contract

Trends

1. Globalization of their market
2. Cost pressures, leading to low-bid policy
3. Their customers demanding better quality/reliability

Key Players

1. Mary Hurley: QC section chief (sponsor)
2. Rich Onoro: Cost-conscious Finance VP (Antisponsor)
3. Len Schneider: VP-Operations (possible Strategic Coach?)

Vulnerability

1. Competitor's new model tester coming out next spring

PART III

Setting Your Strategy

‖10‖

"Knowing What the End Result Looks Like": Strategic Goals

MIT mathematician Norbert Wiener, whose writings on feedback were the foundations of modern systems analysis, used to distinguish between "know-how" and "know-what." It was a lot easier, he said, to develop the former than the latter—yet without "know-what," "know-how" didn't count. To achieve anything of substance, Wiener said, you had to keep the *purpose* of your activity in mind. Knowing *how* to run a machine, a political campaign, or a business enterprise was important, sure. But all the technical or management expertise in the world wouldn't help you if you forgot what you were running it *for.*

In a less esoteric arena, Vince Lombardi once made the same point. John Madden had asked the great Green Bay Packers general to define the difference between a good and a bad coach. Lombardi's response: "It's knowing what the end result looks like. The poor coaches don't have a clear picture of the end. Good coaches do."

What is true in systems theory and football is also true in business. You can have the latest Star Trek production system and the most gut-busting sales force in the world. Neither one will mean anything strategically unless everybody on your account team clearly sees the "end result" he or she is working for—in other words, unless everyone sees where the strategy is *going.*

Like other observers of corporate enterprise, when we speak of "end results," we use the term Goals. Unlike most observers, however, we take a uniquely realistic approach to Goal-setting.

TRADITIONAL GOAL-SETTING: A FOOL'S PARADISE

In establishing "goals"—especially sales goals—most businesses are anything but realistic. Typically they set corporate goals that are impossibly vague ("Increase our market share") while setting sales goals that are just as impossibly precise ("Boost fall quarter revenues by 7.5 percent"). This double confusion leads them, not infrequently, into a fool's paradise of wish fulfillment where true Goals are subordinated to computer-assisted "projections" that bear about as much relation to real end results as the sizzle does to a steak.

In this fool's paradise, the typical "goal" is unrealistic in three ways.

First, it's unnecessarily *quantitative*. Focused to a truly mind-boggling degree on cash-flow charts and market projection specs, businesses attempt to operate by the numbers and to insist that all goals must be *measurable*.

Second, it's generated by *past* rather than current sales realities—so at the very best it can never be more than a sophisticated guess, or "projection."

Third, it's too *self-centered*. Not as in "selfish" or "egotistical," but as in "I can't see why this account won't let us in—don't they see how much we want their business?" Most corporate goal-setting forgets the cardinal rule that the *account* ultimately decides whether or not your goals are met—and that it decides on the basis of *its* needs, not yours.

In this where-you're-going part of the LAMP program, you'll define Goals that avoid these three errors. You'll be able to do so because you'll be following a unique definition: In LAMP strategy, a Goal is a *qualitative* position that the Large Account both endorses and validates.

GOALS: THE QUALITATIVE DIMENSION

Certain Goals are indeed quantifiable. In the next chapter you'll define a distinctively measurable Goal called the Primary Reve-

nue Target. But most business Goals cannot be "counted" in the
same way you count capital expenditures or personnel. This is
rank heresy in an age where ten-year-olds own pocket calculators.
But it's true. You can measure revenue, and payroll, and operating costs. But in the long-term management of Large Accounts,
true Goals do not appear on the spreadsheets.

Part of the reason lies in that familiar phrase, "long term."
Because LAMP defines Goals as desired "positions," and because
solid positioning never happens overnight, we say that the end
results you should be aiming for will typically take a year or more
to achieve. If you're looking at an accomplishment that you expect to tie down in six weeks, chances are it's what we call an
Objective, not a Goal. We'll explain the distinction in more detail
in chapter 16.

Another reason is that Goals are achieved only when your
Large Account agrees they've been achieved—most often because people in that account have met *their* goals. In a sense,
when you lay out your Goals, you're setting your sights on what a
friend of ours calls mindshare—the Large Account's mental commitment to an ongoing relationship with your company. Just as
the validity of your Charter Statement "contribution" and the
level of your business relationship are ultimately defined by the
Large Account itself, indirectly so are your Goals. In fact, a
shorthand way of looking at your Goal is as a link between the
Charter Statement and the buy-sell hierarchy. Meeting a specific
Goal should validate the contribution "promise" of your Statement and by that very fact improve your position in the relational
hierarchy.

To ensure that the element of mindshare is not forgotten, we
say that you should always *write down* your Goals in a specific,
client-centered format—one that emphasizes how *clients* see
you. Let's look at some examples.

"CUSTOMER'S MIND" REVISITED

Recall the Charter Statement that one of our clients drafted in its
targeting of the Aerospace Division of General Aviation. In that
statement, the account team promised to provide "the most accurate electronics testing equipment on the market," so that the

customer could maintain its competitive advantage through improved quality control. Here's the first draft of a Goal that was supposed to deliver on that promise:

> *Goal:* To replace their current "patchwork" in-house quality control system with our more reliable, unified systems approach.

When we read that, we responded: "Good start. But you're looking through the wrong end of the telescope. The way you've phrased the Goal here, we know that accomplishing it will be good for you, but we know nothing about the end results for the customer. Rephrase it so the customer has something to buy into."

The account team went back into a huddle. The second time around, they came up with this:

> *Goal:* To provide the client greater quality control reliability by replacing their patchwork in-house system with our unified systems approach.

That was better. Simply by rearranging the sentence, by substituting "replace" with "provide," and by introducing the critical word "reliability," the team put greater emphasis on the account. But the element of mindshare was still foggy. So we underlined the importance of the customer's *perception* of reality. Strategic position, we said, is always in the mind of the beholder. On its third try, the team produced this copy:

> *Goal:* To be seen by the Aerospace Division as the company that brought them greater quality control reliability by upgrading their patchwork in-house system with a unified systems approach.

This time they had taken our point. Even though the wording changes between the second and third drafts were "minor," they accomplished a critical shift in perspective, moving the focus subtly away from the seller's contribution to the way the customer would *see* that contribution. The value-added "reliability" was important, sure. But the improved position that the team was eventually able to secure in this account didn't come from "reliability" in the abstract. It came from the customer's *perception* of this supplier as the provider of that business result.

Semantics? Don't believe it. We've worked with hundreds of Fortune 500 revenue leaders. Many of them accuse us of playing with words when we insist on the "Be seen as" phrasing—until they realize how this "merely semantic" device helps them see themselves as the account is seeing them. And how such "thinking with the customer's mind" provides a leverage in the account that you can never achieve with the more typical "outside" perspective.

Here are further examples of qualitative, long-term Goals stated from the account's point of view:

- Be known as the firm that helped this account break into the competitive West Coast market.
- Be seen as providing the best follow-up service of any company in our industry.
- Have the account recognize our expertise as the provider of unique solutions to his banking problems.
- Be recognized at the vice president manufacturing level as the best resource for its assembly needs.
- Be seen as delivering more than we promise.

Notice two things about these sample Goals. First, although none of them gets down to measurable nuts and bolts, none of them is vague either. When we say that true Goals are qualitative, we *don't* mean they're wishy-washy or abstract. In the General Aviation example, the Goal hooked up specifically to quality control improvement. In the examples given here, there are also clearly defined business elements: "service," "West Coast market," "banking problems." Like the "contribution" section of your Charter Statement, your Goals should define *specific* ends that relate to your business, the customer's business, and your relationship.

Second, notice that the companies' "end results" all relate to the customer's biggest end result, the bottom line. We'll speak more about bottom-line results in chapter 15, but here's the basic

point: Each of your Goals should fulfill the implied promise of
your Charter Statement to help the customer *run his or her
business better.* It should help the customer reduce *costs*, boost
sales revenue, improve *productivity*, or raise *profit*. A Goal that
doesn't do one of those things—either directly or indirectly—is
probably not a Goal worth pursuing.

We realize that's a pretty strong statement. It's also a very good
guideline. If you can't show a positive impact on your customer's
costs, sales, revenues, productivity, or profits, why would he or
she want to do business with you?

GENERATING GOALS

You can't realistically work toward achieving more than a few
long-term Goals at a time. However, in setting strategy, you
should begin broadly, gradually sharpening your focus toward the
most significant and most viable end results.

To help generate multiple Goals, LAMP teams utilize two
techniques.

The first is creative team thinking. We're strong proponents of
this process, because we believe in the truth of the adage
"There's nothing as dangerous as an idea if it's the only one you
have." Working in an account team, you have a perfect opportunity to think creatively and collectively, generating imaginative, synergistic Goals. In the Strategy Workshop on Goals, we'll
present some field-tested guidelines for doing so.

The second technique is to extrapolate from the Situation
Appraisal Summary—the document you put together in chapter
9. In that summary, you identified fourteen measures of your
current position with your Large Account: three Strengths, four
Opportunities, three Trends, three Key Players, and your single
most significant Vulnerability. Because Goals have to be connected not only to the ends defined in your Charter Statement
but also to the current situation, you'll use the Situation Appraisal Summary both as a catalyst and as a reality check on
possible end results.

In seeking to define realistic Goals, you'll consider these fourteen points *interactively*. The aim is not simply to come up with
fourteen distinct end-results—that would probably not be

realistic—but to define a handful of "best-bet" Goals that incorporate two or more of these critical elements.

If there was such a thing as an ideal Goal, it would incorporate one element of each measure of your position. That is, it would use a unique Strength that could be leveraged through a Key Player to capitalize on an Opportunity that rides a growing Trend—while neutralizing your significant Vulnerability. That's a mouthful, and possibly it happens only in Oz. But it's a good benchmark to aim for. The more clearly your Goals are connected to the realities of your current position, the more likely you are to attain them.

IS THIS GOAL VALID? THE ACID TEST

To summarize what we've said in this chapter, strategic Goals, as we define them in LAMP analysis, are usually *qualitative* rather than quantitative, will probably take a *year* or more to achieve, and are best stated from the *account's* point of view. They are consistent with the contribution you've defined in your Charter Statement and with your Large Account's bottom-line "end results."

Testing your supposed "goals" against these guidelines should help you sort out the real (and realistic) positions your company wishes to achieve from the mere "quick kills" and the pipe dreams. But one test is even more rigorous. It goes back to what we've said about involving the customer, and it's important enough to highlight:

> After you've written down your Goal in black and white, show it to people in the Large Account. If it's a valid Goal, they'll be able to buy into it.

Recall our discussion of the account team that set a Goal to improve General Aviation's quality control. If they had showed the first draft of that Goal to the account, it's unlikely that decision makers there would have gotten behind it: The account's own self-interest wasn't clearly stated. The second draft might have gotten them interested, and the third almost certainly would have. It stated bluntly exactly how the seller wanted to be perceived and what it was going to do to bring that about. It would make perfect sense to show this third statement to the customer: Its "partnership" intention was undeniable.

Of course, once it was shown the statement, General Aviation might still have been skeptical, and with good reason: Seeing a mutually beneficial Goal clearly doesn't guarantee you're going to achieve it. But the customer could hardly have responded with "We don't like this idea" or "This seems like a bad place for you to be." The intention was too solid, for both parties. And that's what Goals are, after all: *intended* positions. Like any other position in LAMP strategy, they need the endorsement of the customer to become reality.

‖11‖

Primary
Revenue Target

We've been emphasizing the qualitative dimension of Goals because quality, not quantity, breeds success. Every successful company we've ever encountered got that way by respecting one fact: It's the sound management of quality relationships, over time, that leads ultimately to a healthy bottom line.

But "ultimately" can take a long time. In the meantime, the troops are hungry, the fax bill is due, and oil just went up fifteen dollars a barrel. While your company is moving up the buy-sell hierarchy, while you're defining and working toward your Goals, you've got to continue meeting overhead costs *and* your payroll. You do that with revenue. And—in spite of what the leveraged buyout wizards might have you believe—the best source of revenue is still your accounts. Most of all your critical Large Accounts.

Because we recognize that businesses run on revenue, we counsel our clients, when they're setting strategies, to define one particular Goal that *is* quantifiable and that hooks up very directly to the revenue stream. We call this Goal the Primary Revenue Target.

YOUR ONE "HARD" GOAL

Most strategic Goals might be described as "soft" in that they don't have a "hard data" component. "Be seen as providing cutting-edge research data to their engineering department." That's clear enough, and quite specific, but there are no *numbers* involved.

Your Primary Revenue Target, on the other hand, is defined expressly in terms of numbers. A uniquely "hard" Goal, it states precisely *how much* of a given product or service you expect to place with your targeted Large Account by a given date. Thus, whereas most Goals are an indication of intended *position*, your Primary Revenue Target is an indication of intended *volume*.

For example, the following Primary Revenue Targets were established by account teams in LAMP workshops:

- "The account will buy 150,000 gallons of our Formula TLC by the end of fiscal year 1992."
- "The Engineering Division will accept shipment of fifty gross units of the Favax transformer by July 1, 1991."
- "This account will sign for $3.75 million worth of billings by the start of Fall Quarter 1992."

Notice that the measures of volume may vary from case to case—you may want to set a Primary Revenue Target for one Large Account in terms of dollar revenue and for another in terms of tonnage shipped—but that, in every case, it's expressed in figures. Your more conservative cipher-jugglers might wrinkle their noses at the concept of Goals, but they'll feel right at home with Primary Revenue Targets.

Notice too that the Primary Revenue Target is *not* exceptional with regard to the other major characteristics of Goals. As with your "softer" Goals, we urge you to set a Primary Revenue Target that is one to three years out from the present. And, as with other Goals, the grammatical emphasis is on what the customer will *buy* rather that what your company can sell him or her. Even when you're forecasting the revenue stream, thinking with your customer's mind is in order.

THE "FORECASTING FOG"

You might think it would be easier to define a hard Goal like the Primary Revenue Target than a soft one like "Be seen as providing cutting-edge research data." Aren't numbers easier to work with than "perceptions"?

Actually, no. Your Primary Revenue Target is basically a sales forecast, and you don't need us to tell you that many sales forecasters make Willard Scott look like Albert Einstein. It's *not* easy to set revenue targets that are realistic and that at the same time provide the appropriate incentives for your people. The fact that salespeople are constantly complaining about their quotas indicates how few companies do it well.

The problems here go beyond the inevitable difference in perspective between the managers who set the quotas and the salespeople who have to meet them. Two scenarios frequently bedevil the estimation of how much revenue an account can generate. Both speak to the fissure in modern organizations between the people out in the trenches and the central office.

Scenario 1: The Extrapolation Trap. In this scenario, rather than performing the kind of meticulous account assessment that you performed in your situation appraisal, the forecaster simply looks at last year's figures and jacks them up by a certain percentage margin. "We did a million four with these guys in '90. We're going for 10 percent growth. So the new target is going to be . . . let's see now . . . a million point fifty-four for this year." Presto! In a perfect example of "rearview mirror" calculation, Merlin the Magician comes up with a revenue target that's quantifiable out to seven decimal places.

But the extrapolated figure may bear little relation to reality. Last year's figures, after all, are just that: *last* year's figures. Any number of things might have happened since they were turned in to undermine, or completely invalidate, the jacked-up projection. The account may now be experiencing internal difficulties that didn't exist a year ago. Overhead or supply costs may have gone up. The firm may be reorganizing. It may be preoccupied with government regulations, or shifting its market focus. In addition, any or all of these things could be happening in *your* company too. A failure to consider such changes—in other words, a failure to keep your situation appraisal up to date—can lead to unrealistically high (or low) sales forecasts.

Scenario 2: "Creative" Forecasting. In a second common scenario, armchair strategists take over completely from the people in charge of the account, designing an attack plan for a nonexistent battlefield. In an article in the March–April 1990 *Harvard Business Review*, George Day and Liam Fahey explain how such "creative" forecasting can foul up a strategy:

> Forecasts are entered into a spreadsheet, and people then fiddle with the numbers. The analyst changes one variable at a time, seeing what happens when the market growth is 1% higher, when gross margin is 2% better, when working capital is cut by $3 million. After several hours of experimenting and testing, the variables become completely disconnected from the original strategy projections.

Result? The forecasts become inconsistent not only with each other but with the real world in which the company operates. And the people who are in charge of actually generating the account revenue—the marketing and sales teams and their managers—have to dance to the fiddling analyst's tune. Sometimes, by herculean efforts, they turn that fantasy into reality. Often they can't. It's too blue-sky for anybody's reach.

The common error in both these scenarios isn't simply a reliance on numbers-crunching—you can't run a business today without some of that. The problem is that, in their zeal to quantify everything, many "data-driven" firms forget the obvious: that the customer's needs affect the value of every figure. If your projections don't hook in to your customer's current situation, it doesn't matter that you've run a "perfect" program. You'll be like the kid who scores 1600 on his College Boards but can't find his way to the post office.

CUTTING THROUGH THE FOG: "BRACKETING"

To help you avoid such blue-sky traps, we recommend that you employ two simple techniques to identify your Primary Revenue Target. First, write down the Primary Revenue Target description from the point of view of the potential revenue *source*, as we've done in the examples just given. Not "We'll sell them 300 units" but "They'll buy 300 units." Like the "Be seen as" formula for phrasing Goals, this device puts the emphasis where it belongs. More so than with any other Goal, it's easy to think of the Primary Revenue Target as *your* business, when actually it's *the client's* business that makes it fly or fall. Putting the client in the grammatical driver's seat helps you keep that in mind.

The second technique is what we call bracketing. Because it's so difficult to come up with a realistic Primary Revenue Target, we urge your team to do so in three steps.

First, pick a Primary Revenue Target that you could achieve if your sales and other resources were *unconstrained*. That's *really* blue-sky thinking. We understand that. But identifying what you could do with the account if you were allowed to go all out helps you visualize a kind of "low-ceiling" fantasy that, paradoxically, is usually *less* fantastic than Spreadsheet Sam's formulas. This is useful in providing "stretch" to your projections.

Second, pick an equally fantastic *low* Primary Revenue Target: the lowest figure that, given probable resources over the target period, all members of your team can buy into. In other words, define the *minimum acceptable* revenue you can settle for.

Finally, look at what's realistic. Come to a consensus on a Primary Revenue Target somewhere between the high and low brackets. Your aim should be to "stretch realistically." You'll have the opportunity to do that in just a moment.

THE QUOTA QUARREL REVISITED

Setting revenue targets in the manner we've just described should lead to sensible and reliable forecasting. But we admit that in the real world, it doesn't always work this way. In the real world your selling people have all got quotas. They probably don't like them, and they probably complain that the managers who set them have lost touch with what's happening in the trenches. They also probably *meet* them, with some regularity.

Given this reality, why bother with setting Primary Revenue Targets? What's the virtue of a revenue forecasting method that seems to ignore (if not confront) the field-tested stick-and-carrot quota system? There are several equally field-tested answers to these questions.

First, quotas are typically set at the regional, branch, or office level. What works, however fitfully, on these microlevels should not be expected to work with any consistency on the macrolevel of account management.

Second, quotas are by nature tactical, not strategic. Most companies require monthly quotas, and even the most strategically minded look to quarters, rather than years, in assessing sales revenue. Focusing on a Primary Revenue Target helps you put all the monthly or quarterly pieces of revenue in perspective; it provides a view of account growth (or shrinkage) that you're liable to miss when you're cranked up to make that last, essential sale by Friday.

Third, the Primary Revenue Target provides a check on the realism of quotas. Quotas that are set without reference to such a strategically valid forecasting tool can be—and often are—wild guesses.

Fourth, and perhaps most surprising, the strategically sound Primary Revenue Target can actually provide greater incentive than the old meet-the-numbers routine. One of the great unsung lessons of the "productivity through people" development of the 1970s was that, when lines salespeople were allowed to set their own quotas, they typically set them *higher* than their managers had. This suggests that a team-generated, long-term forecast such as Primary Revenue Target might provide more challenge to sales forces than the old, "top-down" imposed monthly system.

Finally, by encouraging teamwork, the Primary Revenue Target reduces resentment while increasing synergy and commitment. A team-created Primary Revenue Target, in fact, embodies the best points of that integrated approach to Large Account management that is becoming increasingly critical to sales survival.

We'll discuss that integration in chapter 20. Now it's time for you to implement the lessons of this and the last chapter in a Strategy Workshop that outlines "where you're going."

STRATEGY WORKSHOP 5:
GOALS/PRIMARY REVENUE TARGET

In this workshop you'll define both hard and soft Goals for your Large Account. Your team should be able to complete it in about an hour.

Step 1. Primary Revenue Target.

Begin by establishing the Primary Revenue Target that you wish to pursue for your chosen field of play. In setting this single "hard" Goal, you'll determine a target date between one and three years away, and you'll decide what *volume* you want to achieve by that date. Volume can be measured in revenue dollars, in amount of product or services delivered, or in any other quantifiable way that makes sense to you as a team.

Begin by determining a high, or "resource-unconstrained," figure that can serve as your best possible upper limit. Copy the following model into your notebook and fill in the blanks with the appropriate numbers:

> *High Primary Revenue Target:* If we were resource unconstrained, (field of play) should buy (volume) of (product/service) from us by (date).

The product or service you want to sell this account should be consistent with the "what" you've defined in your Charter Statement. That's the only restriction. *You* decide how your revenue stream is to be managed and which specific products or services can ensure its stability.

Next, follow the model given here to set a low but still acceptable Primary Revenue Target:

Low Primary Revenue Target: The minimum performance with which all team members would be satisfied, given probable resources, is (volume) of (product/service) by (date).

The date here might not be the same one as you established for your high Primary Revenue Target, and the products or services you'll deliver might also be different; the volume almost certainly will be. What's the same is the consensus you need to reach; as we stressed earlier, no strategy element ever gets off the ground unless the entire strategy team can endorse it.

Now compare the high and low and reach a compromise. The "final" figure should be a stretch, but a realistic one. Write it down, following this form:

Realistic Primary Revenue Target: The customer should buy (volume) of (product/service) by (date).

We recommend that you spend ten or fifteen minutes on this step. If you find yourself getting bogged down in hair-splitting, someone should call time and move on. Your realistic Primary Revenue Target, like any other Goal, is an *intended* position. Nobody's going to arrest you if you don't reach it.

Step 2. Creative Group Thinking.

Now take another ten or fifteen minutes to define the soft Goals that you want to achieve with this Large Account. Remember that a true Goal is *qualitative*, that it will take a *year* or more to achieve, and that it should be stated from the *account's* point of view.

Because the generation of Goals ideally involves a great deal of creative thinking, we've found that a group interchange session can be invaluable in helping an account team to define "where they're going." We recommend that you use this technique, and that you "run" a ten- or fifteen-minute session by the following guidelines:

- *Have everyone participate.* The goal of group creativity is to generate a lot of ideas in a short time. That works only when everybody talks. Such participation also encourages buy-in.
- *Move it along.* Having one person serve as both director and scribe can give your session the necessary rapid rhythm. This person should write down, quickly, whatever Goal a team member suggests. When there's a lull in the suggestions, he or she should call on someone or fill in with Goals of his or her own. In spite of their reluctance (and they will be reluctant), people should be encouraged to *keep presenting ideas*, no matter how "foolish" or "irrelevant" their Goals may seem.
- *No criticism.* This ties in with what we've just said. A good creative session generates a *volume* of potentially useful data. Much of that data will prove to be garbage. Avoid the temptation to ridicule. Synergy happens in these sessions because there's an institutionalized acceptance of the offbeat. The director/scribe should enforce that guiding principle.

Step 3. Select.

Now become more selective. Analyze each suggested Goal dispassionately, getting rid of the *merely* offbeat or unrealistic ones. You may find yourself crossing out half or more of what you've written down. You'll also find that comparing "lousy" ideas often generates good ideas you hadn't considered before. Take about another ten minutes for this step, winnowing your list down to the best choices. You may have a half-dozen, or twenty, of these. These are now possible Goals.

Step 4. Organize.

Now turn to the Situation Appraisal Summary that you developed in the last Strategy Workshop. Take the fourteen points that you listed there and transfer them to the "Possible Goals" chart that follows. After copying this chart into your notebook, write in your three Strengths and one Vulnerability in the left-hand column. Then, in the three middle columns, fill in your Opportunities, Trends, and Key Players. You'll have to copy each of these strategic elements four times. You'll end up with a chart that resembles the one shown here.

When you've filled in the first four columns of the chart, you're ready to begin organizing your data. Working with the winnowed-down list of possible Goals and with this new chart, try to define at least one solid Goal for each of your four Opportunities. Write them down in the far-right column.

We've arranged the chart to make it easier for you to do this. Recall that the best possible Goals utilize two or more of the strategic elements. By reading across the Goals chart from left to right, you should be able to perceive connections between these elements that will suggest Goals your group creative session did not reveal. Synergy again, but more organized.

Suppose, for example, that you're the electronics company we introduced a few chapters ago. Among the strategic measures you identified on your Situation Appraisal Summary are the following:

- *Strength.* "The best testing equipment on the market."
- *Opportunity.* "Large Account's concern for quality: testing equipment down for repairs too often."
- *Trend.* "Their customers demanding more reliability."
- *Key Player.* "Quality control section chief Mary Hurley: a Sponsor who wants more reliable service."

After lining up those four elements across the chart, you might come up with the following possible Goal: "Be seen as company that brought them more reliable testing with our unified systems approach."

It won't always work out that neatly. You may not find a distinct Goal for each Strength-plus-Opportunity pairing. In addition, some of your Goals will overlap, and you'll find yourself developing essentially the same Goal for two or three different lines of the grid. That's all right. This is not an exercise in filling in the blanks. The point is to generate as much *usable* information as you can, using the fourteen points as a guide. We've filled in four sample Goals on page 119 to illustrate our point.

POSSIBLE GOALS

Strengths Vulnerability	Opportunities	Trends	Key Players	Possible Goals
Strength #1 Best testing equipment	1. Robotics interest 2. Mexican plant 3. QC problem 4. Subassembly contract	1. Globalization 2. Cost pressures/low bid 3. Customer's quality demands	1. Mary Hurley 2. Rich Onoro 3. Len Schneider	1. 2. 3. 4. 5.
Strength #2 Engineering flexibility	1. Robotics interest 2. Mexican plant 3. QC problem 4. Subassembly contract	1. Globalization 2. Cost pressures/low bid 3. Customer's quality demands	1. Mary Hurley 2. Rich Onoro 3. Len Schneider	1. 2. 3. 4. 5.
Strength #3 Knowledge of their QC problem	1. Robotics interest 2. Mexican plant 3. QC problem 4. Subassembly contract	1. Globalization 2. Cost pressures/low bid 3. Customer's quality demands	1. Mary Hurley 2. Rich Onoro 3. Len Schneider	1. 2. 3. 4. 5.
Vulnerability Competitor's new model	1. Robotics interest 2. Mexican plant 3. QC problem 4. Subassembly contract	1. Globalization 2. Cost pressures/low bid 3. Customer's quality demands	1. Mary Hurley 2. Rich Onoro 3. Len Schneider	1. 2. 3. 4. 5.

Step 5. Validity check.

You now have perhaps ten, perhaps twenty, possible Goals. Be sure each one is phrased in the "Be seen as" pattern that we discussed in the last chapter. Then check each one against two external measures:

First, ask yourself if the Goal you've defined is consistent with your team's Charter Statement. Does each Goal mesh with the "what" you're expecting to deliver in this field of play? Furthermore, does it enhance the "contribution" to the Large Account? If not, it may not be a valid Goal, and you might have to revise or eliminate it.

Second, check to see if your Goal facilitates, or hampers, the attainment of your Primary Revenue Target. Your one hard-data Goal and your several soft Goals are, after all, part of the same general strategy. *They must be consistent with one another.* If putting your state-of-the-art quality control package into this Large Account is going to take three years in itself, while the potential return from that deal is only 10 percent of your anticipated Primary Revenue Target, then something is out of sync and has to be adjusted.

That "something" might not be your Goals. It might be the Primary Revenue Target itself. Or it might be your original Charter Statement. Since the watchword of good strategy is constant reassessment, take this opportunity to review that basic document. Is it still a realistic picture of your field of play? Or does it have to be rewritten in the light of your Goals?

Step 6. Select again.

It would be nice if you could meet all your Goals simultaneously, every year, year after year. But that isn't the way the world works. In setting Large Account strategy, therefore, you start with what your team judges to be the most significant, most crucial, of your Goals—the ones with the greatest likelihood of improving your position in the account and on the buy-sell relational "ladder." Pick *three* to *five* of the Goals you've developed in this workshop. Circle them on the "Possible Goals" worksheet, or write them out on a new page of your notebook. These descriptions of your

POSSIBLE GOALS

Strengths Vulnerability	Opportunities	Trends	Key Players	Possible Goals
Strength #1 Best testing equipment	1. Robotics interest 2. Mexican plant 3. QC problem 4. Subassembly contract	1. Globalization 2. Cost pressures/lowbid 3. Customer's quality demands	1. Mary Hurley 2. Rich Onoro 3. Len Schneider	1. More reliable testing 2. 3. 4. 5.
Strength #2 Engineering Flexibility	1. Robotics interest 2. Mexican plant 3. QC problem 4. Subassembly contract	1. Globalization 2. Cost pressures/lowbid 3. Customer's quality demands	1. Mary Hurley 2. Rich Onoro 3. Len Schneider	1. Research specs for Mexico 2. 3. 4. 5.
Strength #3 Knowledge of their QC Problem	1. Robotics interest 2. Mexican plant 3. QC problem 4. Subassembly contract	1. Globalization 2. Cost pressures/Lowbid 3. Customer's quality demands	1. Mary Hurley 2. Rich Onoro 3. Len Schneider	1. Fix QC problem 2. 3. 4. 5.
Vulnerability Competitor's new model	1. Robotics interest 2. Mexican plant 3. QC problem 4. Subassembly contract	1. Globalization 2. Cost pressures/lowbid 3. Customer's quality demands	1. Mary Hurley 2. Rich Onoro 3. Len Schneider	1. Fix QC problem now — before new entry 2. 3. 4. 5.

team's intention are the most important end results of your developing strategy. They define what you want your position to look like three years from now.

Step 7. The acid test.

As a final test of the validity of your Goals, ask the same question that you asked about your Charter Statement. Would you be willing to show the customer your team-generated and team-approved statement of intent? You're well on your way now in the setting of a strategy for your Large Account, and the end of that strategy is, or should be, a richer and more stable relationship between your companies. You're aiming for partnership as well as productivity. If you're not willing to show your potential partner where you want to go with him or her, you should reconsider your stated Goals before proceeding.

When your team is satisfied that you understand where you're going, move on to the next chapter. It's time to return to Henry Ford's idea of "resource concentration" as the next step toward making your Goals a reality.

‖12‖

Building Your
Own Model T:
Focus Investment

Now that you've decided where you want to go with your selected Large Account, you need to identify which activities are most likely to get you there by the target date. Inevitably this means making choices. Because not even the Japanese have yet come up with a twenty-five-hour day, you must choose to perform certain activities *at the expense of others*. This chapter presents some guidelines for making those choices.

We observed in the introduction that Henry Ford displayed almost fanatical devotion to marketing a single product, the Model T. The concentration of resources that he brought to bear on this endeavor was an excellent example of *focused* effort. In reaching the Goals that you've set for your Large Account, emulating Ford's focus is essential.

The obvious reason is shortage of time. Even if you had no social or family life and spent every waking hour doing business, you'd still be unable to devote all your time to a single Goal or set of Goals. Because you've got various (often conflicting) day-to-day responsibilities, part of your attention will inevitably be deflected from improving your position in any given Large Account.

In addition, resources other than time are also limited. If you could devote unlimited funds, support services, and personnel to

nailing down Goal A for Large Account B, you might reach that
Goal in record time. But the rest of your business would be
gasping for air. As we pointed out in the introduction, when we
speak about concentrating on Large Accounts, we don't mean
tunnel-vision devotion to one client, but rather relative concentration of effort. The same principle operates within each individual Large Account: To stay alive while you're getting to your
Goals, you've got to spread your resources optimally over various
activities.

"SELLING TIME" VERSUS "SALES INVESTMENT"

In our earlier book, *Strategic Selling*, we pointed out that this
applies particularly to your most precious resource, "selling
time." We defined selling time as the time that you devote to
securing individual sales Objectives—pieces of business that you
expect to close within thirty to sixty days. Because our Strategic
Selling program was designed to help you strategize such near-
term Objectives more effectively, in that book we stressed the
management of selling time and said little about managing business time in general.

Because the scope of Large Account strategy is much broader
than thirty or sixty days, we shift the emphasis here. When
you're thinking not "this sale" but "this account," it's equally
important to manage those activities that relate to long-term sales
investments. These are account-related activities whose impact *is
not tied to only one sale or piece of business*.

For example, almost every salesperson we know has spent
time and resources on the following:

- Calls to establish new relationships.
- "Probe" calls to gather information about an account's manu-
  facturing, inventory, or other operations.
- Exploratory meetings to determine a company's divisional
  or regional needs.
- Calls to determine a prospect's level of satisfaction with
  current vendors.
- Lunches, dinners, and golf games with longtime clients.

Often the seller convinces himself or herself that such activities are examples of "selling time." They're not. Because these calls *do not target specific sales opportunities*, you're not really selling when you're on them. They're actually examples of time *investment*, because the payoff for doing them is nonspecific and down the road.

Such social and exploratory interactions may be every bit as valuable as real sales calls. *Any* expenditure of time and resources that helps you position yourself better with your Large Account—whether it happens in a manufacturing plant or over a glass of wine—can make strategic sense. But the time availability for these investments is stretched too, so we're back to the question of resource allocation. Once you set your Goals, which activities will get you there?

CRITERIA FOR FOCUS INVESTMENTS

The question is analogous to the question an investor asks when debating which portfolio to adopt: From which of the available investment opportunities am I most likely to get a high, balanced return over a long period of time? In answering that question, she considers such criteria as current stock prices, past performance, and market trends. Rather than guessing like a lottery or roulette player, she makes an informed wager, trying to minimize her uncertainty, and thus her risk.

That's the smart way to do it. Unfortunately, many businesses, in determining where to place their limited resources, behave not like savvy investors but like hicks in Atlantic City or Las Vegas. Realizing that their available funds are limited, they attempt to cover as many "opportunities" as possible by placing little bets on a dozen different numbers. Occasionally they guess right and go home winners. Usually they get just as flattened by the odds as the chump who plays "hunches" on numbers 7, 14, and 29.

Playing your hunches about which account opportunities will pay off—or, even worse, spreading your people paper-thin over *every* opportunity, no matter how slim—is merely a variation on the theme of "I'm guessing." And account management is too important to be left to guesswork.

Here's the tragic (or maybe comic) part of the scenario. You don't *have* to rely on guesswork to make your choices. Unlike the gambler, you have information that allows you to reduce the risk of the resource investments you make. Not eliminate it—it's not a perfect world—but certainly to make judicious allocations.

We're referring to the account information that you developed in the situation appraisal. There you identified five key strategy elements: Strengths, Opportunities, Trends, Key Players, and Vulnerability. In a Strategy Workshop in the next chapter, you'll apply these criteria to your possible sales activities to define the best Focus Investments for your chosen Goals.

At this point we'll stress just one fact. In focusing resources, you should always *lead from Strength*. When we speak of "focus," in fact, we mean that ideally *all* investments of sales resources for a Large Account should leverage from what your company does well, and should be applied against those problems in the account where your unique Strengths can best provide solutions.

EXAMPLES OF FOCUS INVESTMENTS

Let's consider two examples of how this works in practice. The first is from our old friend, the electronics company that was targeting a manufacturer's quality control department. One Goal that the account team defined was "Be seen as the company that brought them greater quality control reliability by upgrading their patchwork in-house system with a unified systems approach." In moving toward that Goal, the team discovered that the U.S. Navy had recently become this customer's own largest customer. Putting the quality control and navy information together, the account team came up with these two Focus Investments:

1. Provide additional consulting in electronics testing at no charge to their quality control lab.
2. Hire as a consultant a retired account manager from the Large Account to learn how they sell to the navy.

Two observations. First, neither one of these two Focus Investments tied in directly with *immediate* sales Objectives. Thus, there was no "selling time" involved in either investment decision. Second, each decision *did* tie in with one or more of the criteria we've just suggested: Strengths, Opportunities, Trends, Key Players, and Vulnerability. In providing free consulting to the client's lab, the electronics firm worked from a Strength (its superior testing equipment) while targeting an Opportunity (the customer's nervousness about its quality control). In hiring a former Large Account insider, it sought to understand a growing Trend (the increase in navy business) by leveraging on a Key Player, the former account manager. The choice of these two Focus Investments, therefore, was a good example of *informed* resource allocation.

A second example comes from a packaging company's strategy for improving its relationship with a regional grocery chain. In its Charter Statement, the packager's team had focused its attention on "distinctive packaging that increases the sales of in-store–produced bakery products"—the team was seeking to boost the chain's own market share against that of such national giants as Pillsbury and Nabisco. As for Goals, it wanted to achieve two things: "Be recognized as the dominant supplier of eye-catching, innovative packaging." And—because it was poorly positioned with top management—"Get the regional marketing headquarters to understand that we consider them our most important client."

To make optimal use of its resources toward these Goals, the team decided on the following Focus Investments:

1. Hire a top commercial artist with a national reputation and dedicate her to the baked-goods field of play.
2. Provide artistic consulting to their marketing department.
3. Start a program that has one of our executives call regularly on their regional headquarters management.

Again, none of these Focus Investments related *directly* to individual pieces of business. But they all related, very clearly, to the business at large—and to the relationship between the two firms. They also tied in well to our suggested criteria.

- Decisions 1 and 2 played from a *Strength* (the packager's expertise in visual display). They also rode the *Opportunity* of the grocery chain's interest in stealing the Pillsbury Doughboy's thunder.
- Decision 3 sought to neutralize the *Vulnerability* of poor positioning by developing *Key Player* contacts up the hierarchy.

You've probably noticed one other feature common to all these Focus Investment examples. Not one of them was cheap. They were freebies to the customer, but they all cost the investing company heavily, in real time and real dollars. That means, to some degree, that they were painful.

PAY NOW, PLAY LATER

Many companies are reluctant to take on this kind of pain. They'd rather minimize the outlay of Focus Investments in the hope that hard work and a little luck will pay off. In *some* part of the account. Somehow. Some time.

As we emphasized earlier, such a hit-or-miss approach to account strategy almost never pays off in good business. It may seem more comfortable—less expensive, less risky—in the short run. But in a highly competitive atmosphere, the failure to focus your resources on your best Opportunities inevitably leaves you open to account erosion and to the uncertainties of a "strategy" built on chance.

Focus Investments are not guarantees. And we admit that they can be expensive. Expanding your consulting services, hiring a topnotch artist, sending your executives out to call on theirs—none of that is cheap. It's not cheap to buy AT&T stock either. You do so for a good strategic reason. Not because there's *no* risk of losing money. But because, considering all the available information, the probability that your chips will pay your bills is a lot higher with AT&T than with Caesar's Palace or the Taj Mahal.

We've said that the payoff from many Focus Investments

might not come for months, or even years, down the line. Is such a long-term return worth betting on?

The experiences of our electronics and packaging companies say yes. Starting with revenues from their manufacturing Large Account of $700,000 yearly, the electronics company set a Primary Revenue Target of $6 million over three years. With sound Focus Investments, it took them four years, but they reached $7 million. As for the packager, its account team set a Goal of a 150 percent increase in shipping volume; at the end of its target period, it had *doubled* that.

Success is not guaranteed. But one thing is. If you choose to spread your resources thin rather than focusing them, you're taking a far bigger gamble with your company's health than you'd be taking with even the riskiest of Focus Investments.

We'll rest our case with a brief military analogy. Recall the "resource allocation" strategy that George Armstrong Custer adopted on that June day in 1876 when he marched his men into the Little Big Horn Valley. Fearful of missing the Sioux and Cheyenne if he sought them in only one location, he split his forces into three separate columns, each one to cover a different area. The result was that none of the three columns was an effective fighting force on its own. Custer found his "opportunity," all right. Ask Chief Crazy Horse about the results.

‖13‖

"Just Say No":
Stop Investment

One of the most firmly entrenched articles of the corporate sales canon is that you must respond faithfully to *every* request for proposal or request for quotation. Whether the request comes from an account you've done business with for twenty years or an unknown player who gives you forty-eight hours to respond, your company has to follow up the lead. If you don't—so goes the given wisdom—you won't get a shot at the next one, and you'll be nipping future business in the bud. The moral: When it comes to customers, treat everybody alike.

Sounds good. Inclusive, optimistic, and most of all "fair." But it makes absolutely no sense.

Over the combined fifty years that we've been in selling and general management, we've asked hundreds of colleagues a simple question: "How often have you written solid business from an RFP or RFQ that came in at the last minute?" The responses have ranged from "One time in a thousand" to "Never." To anyone who sells in a corporate environment, these are predictable responses. In our guts we know all requests are not alike. We know that when customers ask us to deliver a proposal in two days, they've probably already decided on another vendor and are rounding up last-minute alternates to show their finance departments that they've shopped around. We know that responding to a request for proposal in these conditions has about as much chance of landing business as Saddam Hussein has of running for the U.S. Congress.

We also know about the leads that *do* bring in business, but the kind of business you later wish you'd never written. We've all run into those "irresistible" major orders where the postsale costs in service and damage control make your great revenues look like chump change.

Yet we beat on against the current, trolling for leads—in some cases, jumping into the water after them—even when we know there are sharks below. It's odd but true: Most sales professionals would rather pitch stones against a brick wall than not pitch at all.

We say it's time to stop this nonsense. Our advice for how to deal with obviously marginal or potentially deadly "opportunities" is simple: *Don't.* Let your competition have those thrills. Because your energy and your resources are both finite, focus them where they have a decent chance of paying off. If that chance is merely fair, think about stopping further investment. If it's two steps away from "never," *just say no.*

STOP INVESTMENT SCENARIOS:
FURTHER EXAMPLES

We're not talking only about low-quality leads or unlikely placements to your Large Account. The concept of Stop Investment refers to *any business situation* where you've been investing time, effort, people, and money—and the investment is not paying off.

We're not saying cut and run at the first sign of diminishing or low return. As we stressed in the last chapter, sales investments, just like cash investments, can take time to mature, so sometimes it makes strategic sense to tighten your belt in the hope of future returns. But at other times the account "opportunity" is so littered with danger signals that *not* pulling out becomes an affront to rationality. We advise you to consider limiting your investment especially where one or more of the following scenarios is in evidence:

1. You're on the "outside track." That is, your competition has got the inside track, and no matter how diligently you pursue the business, you're always two steps behind. Perhaps your competition has a unique Strength that you can't match, or your own Strengths are irrelevant to the customer, or the competition has been entrenched in the account for so long that displacing him or her would be seen as home-wrecking. Yes, you should go head to head with your competitors, but only when there's a reasonable chance of a good return. Keeping a presence in the account is one thing; pouring endless resources against an entrenched opponent is quite another.

2. It's not your real business. A friend of ours is a cabinetmaker who creates beautifully crafted period reproductions for a chain of Southwest hotels. Recently one hotel manager asked him to do some small remodeling jobs—plastering and the like—as well. Our friend is capable of performing that work, but it's not his area of expertise, and every hour he spends on a minor trim job is time taken away from his specialty—and from the completion of high-yield projects. On our advice he explained to the manager that he was not in the remodeling business. He would have to decline such requests in the future but would be happy to recommend a handyman whose skills were top notch. The manager couldn't really argue: She ended up with first-rate work in *both* areas.

The lesson: Define the business you want to compete in, and do the best work you can in that field. If you've broadened your efforts to a relatively unknown field and they're draining your resources from more profitable business, it may be time to Stop Investment in this field and to "get back to the knitting."

3. You're flying blind in the Large Account. You can't sell or manage effectively in an information vacuum. Therefore, if you feel—for *whatever* reason—that you lack sufficient information about the impact your efforts are having in a Large Account, it may be time to stop and reexamine the activities you've been focusing on. If you're "feeling your way," if you "need more data," if there have been a lot of "surprises" in handling this business— those are danger signals that should make you wary of getting in deeper.

We don't mean pull back the minute you draw a blank. Obviously the first step to take when you lack information is to try to get that information; LAMP analysis is specifically designed to help you do that. But if repeated attempts to "read" the account leave you still in the dark—if, for example, you still haven't been able to draft a clear Charter Statement or identify active Sponsors or Strategic Coaches—then further "selling" may be a waste of precious resources.

4. New product/new market. An estimated twenty-four out of twenty-five new products fail in the first year after their introduction; when the new product is introduced into a new market as well, the rate rises to ninety-nine out of a hundred. Ask the London-based Wilkinson company. In the late 1960s, this manufacturer of superior garden shears introduced the world's first stainless steel razor in the only distribution network it knew— garden centers. A fine product, but a marketing disaster: Today the market leader's stainless blades *still* outsell the innovator's.

Or take the Aretê Publishing Company, which in 1980 placed an excellent, inexpensive family encyclopedia into an outlet that Britannica and Americana had ignored: retail bookstores. With this new product/new market mix, Aretê soon discovered *why* bookstores had been ignored: Almost nobody walks into B. Dalton's expecting to walk out with an encyclopedia. Ten years after the experiment, Aretê is still short of being a household name.

Trying to place an unknown quantity, trying to crack a new market niche, or trying to create a market for a product that's still being developed—statistically speaking, all of these marketing ventures have a low chance of providing good return. Unless the potential is enormous, and unless your new product is clearly differentiated from what's already out there, it's often smarter to let your competitors break the market, and their necks, with a new offering. At the very least, if you *do* choose to be the first entrant, you should do so aware of the hazards.

5. The money pit. A Hollywood comedy called *The Money Pit* describes the hilarious misadventures of a young couple whose new house, constantly in need of repair, eats their bank account like a black hole eats light. In business it's not so funny. A mining firm once received a court order to clean up the toxic waste from a lake it had fouled; rather than spend the $2 million the cleanup would have cost, it hired a raft of environmental lawyers—and spent ten times that much in legal fees. We know of a landscaping firm that once negotiated for three years with a resort community without getting one inch closer to a contract. And there are of course the famous Hollywood black holes—*Cleopatra*, *Heaven's Gate*—where dogged wastefulness almost ruined studios. In all these cases, the words "No more" were clearly in order.

We've all had money and time sinks in our Large Accounts. The worst ones are prime candidates for Stop Investment. As a rule of thumb, we recommend cutting any project or activity that has already cost you *two* to *three* times its original cost estimate.

These five scenarios are not the only Stop Investment candidates you can run into, and running into them doesn't mean, automatically, that you've got to pull out immediately or lose your shirt. But they are reliable signals to the savvy investor that it may be time to cut losses and say philosophically, "It seemed like a good idea when we started it."

"NEVER SAY DIE": FOUR VERSIONS

It's not easy to get this idea across. In our programs, the concept of Stop Investment generates more controversy, and more resistance, than any other. The fact is that most salespeople, and most businesses, don't like the idea of pulling back. They resist the hell out of it, usually for four related reasons.

The first one we've already mentioned: the sales professional's perennial optimism. As salespeople we're told, from our first days on the job, that a "positive attitude" and "hard work" can work miracles. They can, of course—if they're combined with a rigorous attention to the customer's needs, sound account analysis, and good strategy. Without those pragmatic elements of account management, a gung-ho attitude will get you just about as far as a shoeshine and a smile. Yet the attitude persists. With it goes the self-destructive belief that if you keep plugging away at a piece of business—any piece of business—you'll eventually get it.

Second is the bread-on-the-waters delusion. For many companies, the standard method of developing sales opportunities is the old broadcast method: Scatter your seeds and hope that one out of a hundred turns into a tree. Fine for Johnny Appleseed, but not for business. The idea behind this "philosophy" is that you can't really tell good account opportunities from bad ones, and you shouldn't try. Because selling is fundamentally a numbers game, you should try for *every* order you can get, confident in the ancient sales tenet that "Any sale is a good sale." This attitude, because it leads to force feeding of products and outright deception, has soured thousands of potentially good relationships.

The third version of "Never say die" is "We're already committed, so let's push on." For example: We've already sunk thirty grand into the Green Springs development project. Rather than admitting that this investment was a mistake, let's sink thirty more. Eventually it will all come back. This combination of pigheadedness and gambler's delirium saps the strength of countless businesses every day.

Finally, we hear from our clients that, as much as they'd *like* to kill an unprofitable area of account activity, they're often blocked from doing so by senior management. There's no doubt that this is a major impediment to Stop Investments. Once a marketing objective is enshrined in one of those twenty-pound, holy-writ account plans, it becomes "sanctified" by management approval and in many cases becomes part of the old man's pet marketing scheme—not infrequently because it represents something that worked for him before he became the old man. It takes a lot of fortitude to buck that kind of entrenchment.

A few years ago, for example, we did some consulting with a midwestern food service company whose third largest account was a manufacturing giant. The food service firm ran the cafeteria operations of six separate factories of the manufacturer—and lost money, every year, on every one. This seemed like an obvious candidate for Stop Investment. Yet when we suggested that the food service company should reconsider the wisdom of holding on to that account, we were told that it was the founder's pride and joy—the first Fortune 500 account that he had nailed down himself, years ago. Pulling out might have been judicious, but it still seemed like treason.

THE HARD FACT OF SELLING TRIAGE

We answer all these versions of the "Never say die" argument with the same commonsense observation: *All business is not alike.* Nor are all activities that you perform to pull in a given sale, or position yourself better in a given account. To put a twist on Gertrude Stein's famous observation, "Sometimes a rose is not a rose; it's a Venus flytrap."

An underlying principle of the entire LAMP program is that some accounts have more potential than others—and should be managed accordingly. That works on a microlevel too. Some activities that you perform for your major accounts, some Focus Investments, have more potential than others. Because your resources are limited, you've got to back some and pull away from others. Stop Investment is the essential flip side of Focus Investment.

This means that *some projects must die.* To use a somewhat gruesome but nonetheless accurate analogy, you've got to perform a kind of triage on your Large Accounts and on the Opportunities within them. You've got to decide (1) which Opportunities deserve your immediate and full support, (2) which ones can survive for a while without aggressive management, and (3) which ones are lost causes, bleeding you dry. And you need the courage to *walk away* from this third group.

We *don't* mean "Walk away and let George take over." That's just passing the buck—or, in many cases, the hot potato. If the Baton Rouge plant of the Harrow account has become a money sink, it won't suddenly turn into a cash cow because a different rep, or a different department, is doing your work. When we say drop it, we mean just that: Commit, as a *company*, to pulling out.

We also don't mean "Hang on if there's the ghost of a chance." Hang on if there's a *reasonable* expectation of future income. If the chance is one in a hundred, give it up. Nursing Baton Rouge through a five-year death struggle means ignoring *other*, more salvageable opportunities. It's the hardest lesson the battlefield medic has to learn: Spending an hour with the guy who's almost gone loses him *and the ones who might have been saved.* Yes, it's a grim reality. But recognizing it is a necessary part of being a professional, in medicine *and* in business.

THE HIDDEN BENEFITS OF STOP INVESTMENT

The military analogy makes Stop Investment sound cruel. It's not easy, that's for sure. It goes against every salesperson's gut feelings. It's painful, and cognitively dissonant, and highly irregular. But it's not cruel.

The military analogy, thank goodness, isn't exact. In fact, letting a low-potential Opportunity "die" seldom has a negative impact on the customer, and it almost always improves your company's strategic leverage. Some examples show why.

First, our electronics company. Recall that one of its Focus Investments was to hire a former account sales manager to learn how the account sold to *its* largest account, the U.S. Navy. One Stop Investment that the team defined was to "cease pursuing sales with low potential in the customer's *non*-Navy related business." That's Stop and Focus Investments working together. The team made a conscious decision to *redirect* company resources from low-potential to high-potential activities. You could say that the company "lost" the non-Navy business, but what it really lost was the aggravation that went with it. What it gained was a better buy-sell position—at no extra cost to either organization.

The packaging company tells the same story. Before doing its LAMP analysis, it had sold its grocery-chain account not only "creative" packaging but also plain brown, cardboard shipping cartons. In a LAMP workshop, the team decided that the low return on that Opportunity made it expendable. So members called a Stop Investment on the unmarked cartons—and freed up time and personnel for their Focus Investments, which concentrated resources on their more "arty" lines.

One further example, which illustrates how the supposed "cruelty" of Stop Investment actually encourages *better*, healthier business relationships.

Several years ago a nationwide trucking company totally reassessed its marketing strategy. After analyzing figures from dozens of terminals and regional markets, account executives came to a sobering realization. Over one thousand of their accounts were losing concerns; the revenues they brought in didn't even match operating expenses. Faced with this discovery, company managers called the sales force together and asked them to present a hard choice to their accounts. They were to acknowledge flatly "We can't continue to provide you quality service at current prices. Here's what we *can* offer you." And they were to present three options. "One, we can increase your rates. Two, we can change the mix of your business so we carry your high-yield loads as well as the low-yield ones we're carrying now; with a new mix, we can guarantee your rates *and* our quality. Three, we can shake hands and say good-bye."

Virtually all of the trucker's customers appreciated the salespeople's candor. And over 80 percent of them elected to stay on board, with the altered mix that would make them profitable accounts as well as guarantee them continued service. Far from alienating business by presenting Stop Investment as an option, the trucking company actually strengthened its hold and served the long-term needs of both its customers *and* itself.

The benefits of Stop Investment should be clear from these examples.

- By plugging the time and money drain, it helps you to *conserve* resources that poor investment strategy always wastes.
- It *frees* resources that can be used in better ways. It allows you to *redirect* your time and money for more predictable results.
- If used intelligently, it can *consolidate* your position with valued customers by showing them that you are ready to serve their interests in those areas, and *only* in those areas, where you can do it *best*.

Taken together, these benefits strengthen position in a way that undifferentiated, gung-ho "investment" never can. Let's prove that by reassessing *your* time investments.

STRATEGY WORKSHOP 6:
TIME INVESTMENT

In this workshop you'll define how you can most effectively allocate your limited time and resources toward the achievement of your Primary Revenue Target and other Goals. The picture that you paint here will let you know, in a general way, what activities you should be pursuing with this Large Account over the next two or three years—and what activities you should drop before they drop you.

Step 1. Focus Investments.

Using all the information you've gathered together so far, and utilizing the creative team thinking technique that we described in the previous workshop, identify the areas of activity where your team should concentrate its resources with regard to this Large Account over the next one to three years. Write the heading "Focus Investments" in your notebook, and then complete under it the following sentence:

> We should invest selling time, support time, dollars, and effort in _____.

In defining the most appropriate focus areas, remember that each Focus Investment should tie in to *at least one* of your five investment criteria. So ask yourself:

• What activities can we perform that would highlight for the customer the uniqueness (or "relative uniqueness") of our *Strengths*? Are we sure that this Large Account even understands our uniqueness? Because the best product in the world won't sell itself, do we need to focus more effort on demonstrating our uniqueness to the customer? If we're well positioned in the customer's organizational hierarchy, can we do more to capitalize on that Strength? Are we protecting our Strengths aggressively enough, or do we need to shield them from potential erosion?

• Which *Opportunities* in the Large Account warrant extended sales resource investment because of their long-term payoff potential? Look not only for business that will pay off today, or this year, but for Opportunities that you can "grow" over time. Remembering that the time to buy a stock is when nobody else wants it, ask if there are elements of this customer's business that are in their infancy now, but that might provide solid revenue in the future. Ask: Should we water that seed now, before our competition does?

• The same questions should be asked on the macrolevel. What company-related, industry-related, and broad market *Trends* suggest a more dedicated focus of our efforts? What's happening with this Large Account internally? Are there changes that we can turn to our advantage by a more focused or increased effort? Externally, are there Trends on the horizon that could damage us unless we anticipate their impact? What activities should we pursue to guard against "depositioning from the outside"—that is, "environmental" pressures that might threaten us, the Large Account, or the way we do business together?

• Do we have *Key Players* with whom we could strengthen our position by the careful use of Focus Investment? Investigate Antisponsors as well as the more comforting Sponsors and Strategic Coaches. Neutralizing an enemy by spending time and effort on that person can be just as valuable a contribution to your strategy as nurturing an already good relationship. "Taking a redneck to lunch" may not be as futile as it seems.

• Does our major *Vulnerability* suggest an area that needs to be "backfilled" with more selling time, support time, or other resources? In other words, have we developed this weakness because we've been neglecting activities we *should* have been performing? How can we use our Strengths and Key Players to leverage a Focus Investment against it?

Once your team has identified a half-dozen or so possible Focus Investments, reach a consensus on the *two* or *three* most important ones.

Step 2. Test your decisions.

Now test the validity of these two or three choices by asking yourself two more questions:

• Will following through on this Focus Investment clearly contribute to the achievement of our Goals? Look at both your several "soft" Goals and your Primary Revenue Target. You should be able to draw the same kind of clear links between Goals, Primary Revenue Target, and your Focus Investments as we drew in our electronics company and packaging company examples. You don't need to be able to say "Focusing X more dollars here will get us 39 percent of our Primary Revenue Target." But you should be able to define, to the entire team's satisfaction, how a given activity or resource concentration is likely to pay off.

• Will following through on this Focus Investment strengthen our present *position* in the account? Will it reduce our uncertainty about how the account operates? Move us closer to cashing in on an Opportunity? Improve our relationship with one or more Key Players? Help us get a better foothold on the buy-sell hierarchy? Again, you don't need to prove the link in a mathematical formula. But you should be able to state it clearly—to the satisfaction of everyone on your team.

Step 3. Stop Investments.

Now perform the less comfortable, but equally necessary, "flip side" of time investment strategy by getting rid of those activities that won't pay off. Whether they jump out at you or not, they *always* exist. To bring them to the surface, ask the following:

• What activities are we involved in where we lack a unique Strength advantage, or where that advantage is not clear to the Large Account? Good strategy always starts from Strength: If your competitor has an inside track in a given area, it may be best to leave that area to him or her for the time being and compete where you're stronger.

• Are we not expert in any portion of the Large Account we're targeting? Do we lack the experience to compete effectively in any portion? Is there any area where what we're being asked to do is drawing valuable resources away from areas in which we can perform better? Are we operating to maximum effect in our own defined market, or have we gotten too far away from the knitting?

• In what areas are we flying blind? Where, in spite of all our information gathering, are we still feeling our way, without sufficient data? Where have there been a lot of surprises, mostly negative in impact? Where is it time to see the Big Muddy for what it is, cut our losses, and pull out before we drown?

• Are we trying to sell a new product, or an old product into a new market? The best product in the world hasn't got a chance if the timing of market entry is premature. Are there areas where we should step back, let the competition take the heat for "opening" this slice of Large Account business, and consider reinvesting at a later time?

• What activity or project has been a time and money sink? Where have we been throwing good money after bad—and good time after bad—for too long? Although there's no hard and fast rule for identifying such black holes, remember our suggested rule of thumb: If you've gone two to three times over the original estimate, no matter how good the business *could* be, you may already have paid too much up front.

When you've uncovered areas of possible Stop Investment, agree on the *two* areas that are doing you the most harm. Write them down and commit, as a team, to squander no more resources in that direction. If you can identify more than two investments that should be dropped, fine. But two losers is the bare minimum.

Step 4. Redirect the focus.

Finally, make an informed estimate of how much time (or money, effort, or other resources) your company is likely to *save* by eliminating these two dropped investments. Forget about the calculators and the regression analyses. Just get a gut, consensus reaction about the *increased* investment opportunities that are now open to you with the elimination of the time and money drains.

Where does it make sense to *redirect* this newly available

company resource? Look at your Focus Investment choices once again. How does the release of formerly locked-up resources affect them? Does the windfall suggest *other* Focus Investments—ones you may have considered too costly up to now? Revise your Focus Investment list as your team sees fit, based on the new allocation of resources.

Once you've done that, you can put it all together a second time, in a Draft Strategy for where you're going in your Large Account.

Putting It All Together

STAGE TWO:
YOUR DRAFT STRATEGY

In this Strategy Workshop chapter you'll pull together everything you've surfaced so far, drafting a tentative, one- to three-year strategy for the field of play in your Large Account. By the end of the workshop, you'll have a one-page picture of where you intend to position yourself with this account and in general terms what activities will get you there. Since you'll be organizing rather than uncovering data, this part of the process shouldn't take long. We suggest that you set aside thirty minutes.

STRATEGY WORKSHOP 7: DRAFT STRATEGY

Step 1. Review and revise.

In previous workshops, you've produced three strategic documents: your Charter Statement, your Situation Appraisal Summary, and your Possible Goals chart. Review them now in light of your Focus and Stop Investment decisions. Your new understanding of time investment could dictate modifications of any or all of those documents.

For example, when our electronics company decided to stop investing in its client's nondefense business, its team had to redefine its field of play; an entire arena that team members *thought* they should be attending to suddenly became less relevant. When the packaging company decided to dedicate a commercial artist to its grocery-chain Large Account, it instantly acquired both a Strength and a Key Player that its situation appraisal hadn't identified. Redirecting resources away from generic carton sales subtly changed the nature of its Goals, and—not so subtly—its Primary Revenue Target. In both cases, revision was in order.

When you've agreed upon a new shape for these three documents, write the heading "Draft Strategy" at the top of a notebook page and then write down the following critical items: your revised Charter Statement, four best Opportunities, three most important Goals, and Primary Revenue Target.

Step 2. Pick your best Opportunity.

Now select the *one* Opportunity that has the best chance of getting you to your Goals. This is a judgment call. By definition, *all* of your four best Opportunities have payoff potential, so the single "best" one may not be an obvious choice. There may be disagreement among members of your team. Nevertheless, we recommend that you spend no more than five minutes on this step of the workshop before coming to a decision. Eventually you'll be going after all of your best Opportunities; selecting one now doesn't deep-six the others, and it's better to start *somewhere* immediately rather than waste valuable time debating direction. Write down the consensus choice.

Step 3. Identify the resources needed to ensure success.

Describe briefly what resources you need to concentrate on this Opportunity to *ensure* its success. You don't need to get too specific in terms of scheduling, personal accountability, and the like—we'll get to that in the next part of the book—but you should be able to define, in consensus fashion, what *types* of resources (sales, support, data processing, research, budget, management tie-in) are needed to secure this Opportunity as well as what level of *increase* (in money or time) is essential.

An important clarification. We're *not* saying "List the resources that are currently available for this Opportunity." We're saying "List the *resources it will take to do the job*." Don't try to sketch out your best shot. Rather, identify the Focus Investments that can most predictably improve your position in this Large Account. Spell out, without quibbling, how much that will cost. You may have to do internal selling to release the needed funds, but there's no percentage in assuming you're broke before you begin.

Step 4. "Just say no."

Identify the *least* valuable of your Opportunities in this account—the one least likely to get you closer to your Goals. It probably won't be one of the "four best" that you identified in your Situation Appraisal Summary, although it could be. Be as ruthless as you can in identifying this false friend, and *kill it*. Now. Regardless of how much time and money you've already invested in this Opportunity, make a conscious decision to cease further investment. Define precisely what your team means by "investment"—service functions, human resources commitment, loss leader proposals, or anything else that's consistently failed to pay off—and write that in under "Stop Investment." When you've finished this step of the workshop, your Draft Strategy will look something like the model on the next page.

Step 5. Redirect your resources.

Having freed up resources from your Stop Investments, consider where to shift your time and money focus to ensure the best possible returns from all the remaining Opportunities. The lion's share of the total investment package, of course, will be directed to your single best Opportunity. What about the rest? Your team needs to determine, in a general sense, where to put the remainder of your company's account resources, so that the Large Account as a whole, and not just your best Opportunity, is well served.

DRAFT STRATEGY

Charter Statement:

We provide Aerospace Division with most accurate testing equipment on market, so they can improve their quality control and thus maintain competitive advantage.

Four Best Opportunities

1. Their interest in robotics
2. Opening of new Mexican plant
3. Quality control problem needs fixing
4. Their subassembly contract

Three Best Goals:

1. Help put Mexican plant on line by providing research specs to their planners.
2. Show them they'll get better price/performance with our testers.
3. Bring them more reliability with our unified systems approach.

Primary Revenue Target

$120 K in E19 calibrators by May 30.

Single Best Opportunity

Quality control problem that needs fixing

Focus Investment (Resources Needed)

- Our research people to do systems analysis
- Take Mary Hurley and department to Geary plant, where our QC system is a showcase operation
- Place pilot test program

Stop Investment

In-house telecom system

There are no right or wrong answers here, and certainly no optimum distribution pattern. You want to analyze how the general "flow" of account resources is going to shift, based on the strategy you've devised and the Goals you want.

Step 6. Test your Draft Strategy.

The pieces you've put together comprise a Draft Strategy for your targeted Large Account. Test that strategy now by asking yourself the following questions:

1. *Strengths.* In this strategy, are our company's unique Strengths focused on Opportunities? What specific and unique Strength is focused on the Opportunity we've selected as "best"? Spell it out: "Our Strength as low-bid supplier of the Favax transformer meets their need for an inexpensive component on the Wilkins project." "Our track record of on-time delivery feeds perfectly into their new Just in Time inventory system."

2. *Opportunities.* Are we sure that we've selected the single *best* Opportunity? It's not necessarily the one that will bring the most revenue right away. Look for the Opportunity with the clearest link to one- to three-year Goals.

3. *Trends.* Does this strategy go with the dominant Trends or against them? If we're selling to a Large Account that's on a growth swing, are we positive we can meet their increased demand? If, on the other hand, we're selling to a company that's experienced setbacks, or is nervous about supply shortages or government regulations, full-speed-ahead proposals may not be in order.

4. *Key Players.* Does this draft strategy make efficient use of Sponsors and Strategic Coaches? Does it include contingencies for neutralizing—or at least confronting the objections of—Antisponsors?

5. *Goals.* If we accomplish our Goals, will all members of our account team feel that they have "won"? Will the Key Players in the Large Account feel that *they* have won? How? Document this too. "Jeff Barnes needs better up-time to get back on schedule." "Mary Hurley is eyeing this account as a showcase sale."

6. *Focus Investments.* Are we sure that all Focus Investment

activities have a clear and logical relation to our Goals? What about support programs? Sales and support energy that is not Goal-related may not be appropriate for this strategy.

7. *Stop Investments*. Are we committed to ceasing investment in the one Opportunity that we see as having the lowest return potential? Not "cutting back" or "passing the buck," but *stopping*.

When you can answer these questions to your team's satisfaction, you'll have a solid, general (and general's) map of where you're going. We turn now to *how* you're going to get there.

PART IV

Implementing Your Action Plan

‖15‖

The Key to Implementation: Planning

Throughout this book we've stressed the value of big-picture thinking and the development of a long-term perspective. It's time to shift gears. Because achieving your long-term Goals happens not instantly but incrementally, you also need to focus on the near term, answering questions that relate to more immediate Objectives. What specifically are you going to try to accomplish this quarter, or in the next six weeks? When should each individual task be completed, to keep you on schedule toward your Goals? Who should be responsible for each task? How do you track your progress toward the "end results"?

In short, how do you put your Draft Strategy into *operation*?

PLANNING, PROCESS, AND PROGRESS

To answer near-term questions of this sort, your account team needs to do planning. We say "do planning" rather than "make a plan" because operationalizing a strategy must be dynamic. The last thing we want you to spend your valuable time on is creating a static, phone-directory–size account "plan." By the end of the implementation part of the book, you'll have created a one-page document called an Action Plan. It will be as flexible as most account plans are stiff and as lean as most of them are obese.

The dynamic nature of strategic planning reflects our continual emphasis on process. In fact, we go so far as to say that the process of planning is more important than the finished document you create through that process. You've seen evidence of that in previous workshops. You'll see more as you create your Action Plan.

But process is futile unless it gets you somewhere. For that reason, planning must also be connected to *progress*. The late great Alabama coach Bear Bryant used to say "Have a plan for everything. You'll know if it was right by the scoreboard." Exactly. Plenty of businesses say they have a plan (for market penetration, overhead reduction, or whatever), but when you ask managers how it's working, they can't tell you. That's not a plan; it's a wish list. The only way to know that you really do have a plan is if you can measure your progress against it.

We incorporate these two essential principles into our definition of an Account Plan:

> An Account Plan is a flexible schedule for allocating resources to specific Objectives, with provision for feedback and repositioning toward your Goals.

"Repositioning" and Goals you've already heard a great deal about. We'll be discussing the near-term elements of this definition—putting resources to work on individual Objectives—in this and the next chapter.

WHY PEOPLE RESIST PLANNING

As essential as planning is to account strategy, it's not an easy concept to accept. Salespeople especially fight against it, usually for one of two reasons.

Some of them say it's too time-consuming and/or too difficult to do effectively. There are so many imponderables in selling to major accounts, they say, that planning is an exercise in futility. It's smarter to plug ahead, meeting obstacles as they arise, than waste time plotting out a future that may never happen.

A friend of ours calls this the "Invisible Troll" argument. The salesperson is like the knight in the fairy tale. He decides not to bring his sword with him because there might *not* be a troll under the bridge: no point planning for things that might not happen. And he gets cut off at the knees when they do happen.

Others resist planning because the "plans" they've made in the past have functioned less as aids to action than as straitjackets. Planning by its nature limits responsiveness, they say. Solution? Get "nimble," think on your feet, roll with the punches. Or, as a boxing enthusiast once told us, "Don't get into the ring wearing handcuffs."

On the surface this sounds like good advice. But the analogy is inexact and misleading. What both of these objections boil down to is that there's no point in having a *rigid* plan—one that's unresponsive to changing events. No kidding. We're as dead set against rigid plans as any swordless knight or handcuffed middleweight. But good planning doesn't have to be that.

In fact, one sure sign that your planning has gone awry is that the plan can't be modified as "imponderables" arise. A good plan has feedback and flexibility built in. It sets out clear Objectives, allows for the unpredictable, and adjusts the course setting as those Objectives are (or are not) achieved. It's a kind of account-based management by objectives, with a high degree of responsiveness. And no rigidity.

We sympathize with those who find most "planning" pointless. Unfortunately, the alternatives are even worse. You may remember Winston Churchill's quip about democracy. It was a "very bad system" of government, he said—"except for all the rest." The same point could be made about the account version of management by objectives that we're proposing. Consider the alternatives.

AN ALPHABET SOUP OF ALTERNATIVES

If you don't like our sales version of management by objectives, try one of the following on for size. We've seen all of them in "operation," spinning things out of control.

MBS. Management by subjectives. Otherwise known as the seat-of-the-pants approach or management by intuition. It derives from the "positive attitude" school of thought and leaves virtually everything in the account up to chance. We appreciate "creative thinking" as much as anyone, but you need an enormous amount of luck to make MBS work. Essentially it says "We'll work *something* out." That's not a plan, it's a prayer.

MBE. Management by extrapolation. This translates as "More of the same," "Keep on trucking," or "If it ain't broke, don't fix it." MBE is a popular nonmanagement approach in businesses that have established a dominant share of an account and don't want to risk losing it by analyzing how the business got that way. In an environment where the road is mostly twists and turns, that's an invitation to drive into a wall.

MBC. Management by crisis. Also known, especially in start-up organizations, as the Saturday night poker game approach: "Shuffle and deal again, Charlie." In this completely reactive style, you manage things only when there's trouble. Great for generating excitement. Terrible for achieving even a modicum of continuity.

MBH. Management by hope. Positive attitude again, with a vengeance. Hope some new leads turn up. Hope we can stall the bank. Hope the price of oil doesn't rise. Hope you have a nice day. It's beneath contempt as a "management" or "planning" style. But that doesn't mean there aren't businesses run this way.

The problem with all of these alphabet-soup approaches to management is that they forfeit account control to external forces. By allowing the manager to focus on everything *but* clear Objectives, they ensure that activities will be haphazard and progress unmeasured. A typical result of these alternatives to planning is for a company to rationalize whatever happens as what it wanted to accomplish all along. That kind of management by acceptance (not to be confused with the usual MBA) is what puts many businesses *in* the soup.

WHEN TO PLAN: FIVE SCENARIOS

There are countless reasons to plan, depending on the account, on your business, and on the environment. Planning is particularly important, however, in five scenarios:

1. When the activity you're contemplating is too *complex* or too *important* to be managed by luck or memory. That's true of many activities in Large Account management, and *most* activities of a strategic nature. You may not need a plan to remember your Tuesday meeting with the Nashville branch manager. You definitely *do* need one to arrange a series of briefings for all branch managers in the southern region.

2. When the efforts of other people need to be *coordinated.* This speaks to the team-centered approach of LAMP as a whole. Maybe, if you're a one-person organization, you can get away with a quickie, thinly documented plan for placing newspaper ads. Maybe. If you've got an advertising department, though, you'd better not try. Most activities in Large Account management involve the effort of more than one person: Making sure the right hand knows what the left one is doing requires planning.

A negative example illustrates how the absence of planning can lead to a left-hand versus right-hand fiasco. The city of Santa Fe recently authorized the restoration of some historic buildings in the middle of the downtown shopping district. At the request of the municipal Planning Design Commission, the architect faced the buildings with iron balconies in an agreed-upon early territorial style. But the commission failed to include in its "planning" any of the many other government departments that might legitimately have had a say in the decision. As a result, when the balconies went up, the architect discovered that the Finance Department wanted to levy a stiff penalty for his use of city "air space," while the City Council—which you might have thought would have supervised the decision—declared that the balconies posed a liability for the city and had to be closed off immediately. The entire city government, rightly, became a laughingstock— because of a quite avoidable lack of coordination.

3. When the *commitment* and *accountability* of other people is essential to the accomplishment of Objectives. If Trent has got to call Willis by next Friday, or if Marie has to get you product specs by the end of the month, both of those things need to be spelled out—in writing—to ensure that they'll happen on time. A good plan does just that: It spells things out. What, when, how much. And who's responsible.

4. When your boss *wants* you to. No subtlety here. It's important to keep the head honchos happy. So if the operations vice president asks for a statement of your Objectives and how you'll get them, deliver it. The negative benefit of doing so is obvious: It keeps the V.P. off your back. The positive benefit is even more important: It facilitates the meshing of top-down and bottom-up involvement that is critical to Large Account management.

5. When it's important to track *results*. This covers nearly every scenario that you're likely to encounter with your Large Accounts, because tracking lets you know, while there's still time to do something about it, whether you should increase your resources, decrease them, or modify your plan. More on this when we discuss Milestones in chapter 16.

When we say you need to plan as a means of tracking results, we're thinking of two different, but related, kinds of results.

The first kind you've been looking at all along: the "end results" that we call your strategic Goals. Testing your Objectives against those results is a major function of planning, and you'll be doing that throughout the next three chapters.

It's also important to track, and deliver, the *account's* results— that is, the ends that the account's decision makers want to achieve by doing business with you, or with your competition. This concept requires clarification.

DELIVERING "CORPORATE" RESULTS

Businesses exist to make a profit. They may also make ships, shoes, or sealing wax. But the reason for their existence is profit. Period.

This fact has tremendous significance for account planners, because most if not all Large Accounts are businesses with this essential profit orientation. It's an orientation based on self-preservation. Whatever other concerns may animate the various people in the business organization, the dominant concern of the business at large has got to be profit. Without it, everything else grinds to a halt.

The following diagram shows, in an admittedly simplified

fashion, the kind of things that matter most to organization members as you move up the chain (or in this diagram, the pyramid) of command. At the foundation of the corporate pyramid, the issues of concern are jobs and work quality. As you move higher, departmental agendas and related projects start to take precedence. Middle management worries about sales, costs, and production. And the people at the most senior levels see the bottom line: the heartbeat of profit.

Why should you be aware of this structure as you implement an Action Plan? Because it's the people at the top—the organization's *economic* planners—with whom your company has to be positioned over the long run, if you're going to move from individual Objectives to solid Goals. *To position yourself effectively at that level, you've got to deliver results that match their concerns.*

Specifically, you've got to address the three areas shown in the diagram that *lead* to steady profit. It's imperative that you:

- Improve the *sales* of the Large Account. Not your sales to the account; its sales to *its* customers.
- Reduce its operating or other *costs*.
- Raise the level of its *productivity*.

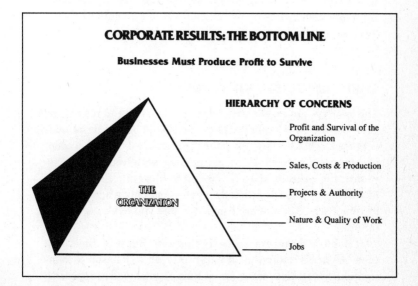

CORPORATE RESULTS: THE BOTTOM LINE

Businesses Must Produce Profit to Survive

HIERARCHY OF CONCERNS

THE ORGANIZATION

Profit and Survival of the Organization

Sales, Costs & Production

Projects & Authority

Nature & Quality of Work

Jobs

Whatever else your individual sales might do, their *strategic* value rests to a great degree on how well they tie in to these interests. Sales, costs, productivity, and profit are the only results, in the end, that really count.

Two implications. First, in planning for Objectives, you've got to position each Objective as closely as possible to bottom-line results for the organization. A computer system that streamlines a Large Account's internal communications network may be seen as attractive by the personnel and data processing departments. Every secretary and section chief in the operation may love it. But unless senior management sees it contributing to profit and survival, it probably will not help your long-term positioning in the account. To survive the ups and downs of today's market madness, you *must* tie your Objectives to the race for profit.

Second, aim high. Don't ignore *any* of the individuals who might impact, positively or negatively, on a given sale. But target particularly those individuals who care most about the company's bottom line. Not only are these senior managers most likely to be "sold" by the profit impact of your proposals. They're also frequently the source of final approval—the types of managers who, in our Strategic Selling programs, we refer to as Economic Buyers. Finally, they're the people whose perceptions matter most in establishing your position in the buy-sell relational hierarchy.

THEIR RESULTS—AND YOURS

The two types of results we've described—your end results and your customers' Corporate Results—should never be at odds with each other. In fact, since the ultimate Goal of good account management is to create a partnership with your Large Accounts, their results and yours ought to be identical. You ought to achieve your Goals precisely when—and only when—people in your Large Account are convinced that you're also achieving theirs.

It doesn't always track exactly this way. But over time, in a good business relationship, it gets pretty close. Johnson & Johnson's chief executive officer, James Burke, put it well in a speech a few years ago: "The businesses that do best over time—that is, that sustain consistent levels of steady profit—do so because they follow a simple imperative: to serve their customers' needs better than the competition."

That "simple imperative" is the heart of every thriving business. The fact that it's too important to leave up to chance is the bottom-line reason you need planning.

16

The Stepping-Stones of Your Strategy: Setting Objectives

Back in the madcap 1960s, when "happenings" were popular in San Francisco, a precursor of today's performance artists announced that he was going to push a grand piano through a circular hole six inches wide. Tickets were sold, the press assembled dutifully, and on the appointed day the artist appeared on stage. To his left, sure enough, was a grand piano. To his right stood a thick wooden wall, in the center of which had been cut a six-inch hole.

For the next three or four hours, using a fire ax, a sledgehammer, screwdrivers, pry bars, and a chainsaw, the artist turned the piano into splinters, and pushed them, one by one, through the hole. For several months after this episode, the Bay Area hummed with this exchange: "How do you get a piano through a keyhole?" Answer: "One splinter at a time."

The probable looniness of the artist aside, there's a pragmatic lesson to be learned here. With enough energy and imagination, the most grandiose and seemingly impossible goals can be achieved—if you work toward them "one splinter at a time."

Tom Peters and Bob Waterman made the same point in their management classic, *In Search of Excellence*. After listening to a presentation on "strategy" by an especially effective corporate line manager, they concluded that his strategy broke down to "a series of pragmatic actions"—the kind of manageable small-scale problem-solvings that they came to refer to as "chunks."

> One year a blitzkrieg group came through from regional headquarters and helped get receivables under control. Another year, the attack was aimed at closing down some unprofitable segments. In another year, a further blitz effort helped work out a novel arrangement with distributors. It was a classic example of the "theory of chunks" . . . The key success factor in business is simply getting one's arms around almost any practical problem and knocking it off—now.

A different kind of piano-smashing, but the same lesson: Start small; get it done; move on.

Getting things manageable so they can be "blitzed" is also the lesson of what we call Objectives. In this chapter we'll be speaking about these account management equivalents to the artist's splinters and the line manager's chunks.

OBJECTIVES VERSUS GOALS: THE DISTINCTIONS

The terms "goal" and "objectives" are frequently confused by businesses that define neither one with precision. Often, in fact, the two are used interchangeably. We distinguish between them in a straightforward and pragmatic manner. Goals, as you've already seen, are the end results of a strategy: They're the qualitative, long-term positions that you intend to achieve in your Large Account. Objectives happen along the way. They are the individual, near-term accomplishments that, taken together, help you reach your Goals. As a rule of thumb, we say that a Goal takes one to three years to achieve, while Objectives should be reached in one year or less.

But the difference in time scale is only one distinction. To illustrate some equally important ones, we'll return to our electronics company.

You'll remember that one of this company's Goals was to be seen as the supplier of greater quality control reliability. To meet that Goal, the account team drafted several Objectives. This was one of them:

By September 15, 1991, we'll place ten of our Model E19 calibrators in their quality control lab, so they can test the Fall Quarter production samples more accurately, thus reducing their retest time and operating costs.

The example illustrates several important points.

First, a Goal defines a position you want to attain. An Objective spells out *how* you're going to get there: It defines the "on the way" implementation of the Goal.

Second, an Objective is more *specific* than a Goal. Goals describe the business relationship you're trying to develop with a Large Account; Objectives describe the particular products, services, or "deals" that will contribute to developing that relationship. Not any "testing equipment," but "Model E19 calibrators."

Third, while Goals are essentially value judgments and thus difficult to quantify, Objectives must be *measurable*: They state volume, percentages, dates, and so on. You always draft Objectives in terms of numbers: *ten* units by September *15*.

Fourth, while Goals are defined from the customer's perspective, Objectives are defined from yours. A Goal says how you want to be *perceived* by the Large Account; an Objective describes an *action you will perform*. In our LAMP programs, we ask that participants phrase their Objectives so that the team or company's action stands out clearly: "We will install." "We will deliver." "We will place."

Fifth, even though the thrust is on your action, the Objective never forgets the customer's needs. Every well-defined Objective identifies the Corporate Results that will happen for the customer when the Objective is achieved. Remember that such Results always relate to sales, productivity, costs, or profit. In this example it's reduction of the customer's operating costs.

One final distinction. Objectives, unlike Goals, are *assigned*. Specific people are responsible for their execution. The responsibility for meeting Goals, almost by definition, is teamwide. But since Objectives are *scheduled* and *concrete*, individual people have got to see that they happen, the way they're supposed to happen, and on time. When the electronics company's account team transferred the preceding Objective into their

Action Plan, they specified, in writing, who was responsible: "Jess Leary's group to coordinate this sale."

THE HIDDEN VALUE OF OBJECTIVES: INCENTIVE

The basic value of setting and meeting Objectives is that it enables you to move toward your Goals in a concrete and incremental fashion; Objectives serve as stepping-stones toward end results. But there's also a less obvious advantage.

It's an interesting fact of human psychology that the closer we get to our major goals, the less compelling they become as day-to-day incentives. This becomes evident as people advance in their careers and the visions that drove them as youngsters—whether they're as specific as making the first million by age thirty-five or as vague as "having it all"—are mellowed by reality and (paradoxically) by success. We've all known hard-driving business professionals who, after thirty years of accomplishments, virtually retire on the job because they've run out of worlds they can conquer. "I've been top gun since Kennedy was in office," they say. "Attaining next year's sales revenue targets doesn't have the same importance that it once did for me." If you're a football fan, you'll notice a similar kind of "summit letdown" in the often-noted Super Bowl slump and the notorious Heisman Trophy "curse": People who have achieved their major goals frequently run out of steam.

But this same burnout phenomenon seldom happens when the target is a near-term "chunk." In fact, just the opposite occurs. The closer we get to achieving immediate, circumscribed aims, the *more* compelling they become. And the harder we'll work to accomplish them.

A terminally bored salesman of the year, for example, won't come into the office on Saturday to "be seen as the dominant supplier of test equipment over the next three years" (a Goal). But if he's at 97 percent of his quota (an Objective) one week away from the quarter's end, he's going to find that old fire in his belly and work like hell to close the immediate gap. The lineman will block harder and the wide receiver will run faster when they're only fifteen yards away from *today's* touchdown.

This psychological fact has an important implication for account management. Although it's critical to keep long-term Goals in mind as you set, and reset, account strategies, to make those Goals operational, you've got to concentrate on near-term horizons. The over-the-horizon end results may (indeed, should) inspire you. But the incentive for putting one foot in front of the other now always comes from today's and tomorrow's doables.

The reason is feedback. We have a friend who tried to lose weight for fifteen years and failed consistently because the goal he set himself was so far out: "Three years from now," he told us at the beginning of one of his many weight-loss programs, "I'm going to look like Tom Cruise." No amount of dieting and exercise did him any good, because three weeks into a new program, he'd check the mirror, fail to see any movement toward his distant benchmark, and give up. No feedback; therefore, no incentive.

Finally he started setting himself small Objectives: "Lose five pounds by the end of this month." "Do thirty sit-ups a day for four weeks." "Cut this week's calorie intake by 10 percent." Every time he reached one of these near-term, doable aiming points, he got the positive feedback he needed. Within three months he had dropped eighteen pounds. (And wisely modified his Goal. Now he wants to look like Paul Newman.)

Goals and Objectives work together. You've got to know what the end result looks like. But to get there, keep your eye on the ground.

FROM "DOABLE" TO "DONE": MILESTONES

Establishing doable Objectives doesn't guarantee that they're going to be achieved. So we recommend, when you define these stepping-stones, that you also establish "minischedules," to see whether the "doable" is becoming the "done."

To facilitate this process in LAMP workshops, we urge the establishment of checkpoints we call Milestones.

A milestone, on ancient Roman roads, showed travelers how far they had gone on a journey between two given points. If they hadn't reached, say, milestone number XII by midday, they knew they'd have to step up the pace to make the Tuscany Taverna, at milestone number XIX, by nightfall. Thus Roman milestones, by allowing travelers to check their progress, also provided the opportunity for corrective action.

LAMP Milestones serve the same function: They allow you to see how *much* of a given Objective has been achieved and where, if anywhere, you need to modify what you're doing to ensure that the whole "chunk" gets done on time.

Take the Objective that was established by the electronics account team: to sell ten calibrators by September 15. Reaching that Objective can't happen all at once. It will involve numerous meetings, phone calls, and en route sign-offs before the calibrators actually arrive in the quality control lab. All those pieces of the deal must be scheduled, and they must be assigned to individual people to ensure accountability. A schedule of Milestones for this Objective might include items like the following:

- July 1. Jen King to call on quality control section chief.
- July 15. Tony Mustelli to verify introductory discount specs with Jess Leary.
- August 3. Demonstration meeting at their Nor-Tex facility. Jen and Jess.
- August 5. Tony to present contract for legal review.
- August 30. Last day for legal approval. Tony to report to Jess.
- September 5. Jen gets sign-off by their VP Finance.

And so on. There might be a half-dozen such en route checkpoints, or many more. Obviously, the more complicated the sale, and the more people involved, the more important it is to itemize schedules and responsibilities. But even the smallest and "surest" sales Objective can be made more manageable (and surer) by such checking.

It's important that this checking be followed up by corrective action when necessary. If Tony hasn't gotten the discount specs to Jess by July 15, your planning needs immediate adjustment. That may mean extra phone calls, extra meetings, to find out what's slowing the schedule. Or (worst-case scenario) it may mean resetting the Objective deadline itself. But some reaction to the missed Milestone is essential, if you want the taverna to still be open when you get there.

It comes back to the *dynamic* nature of strategic planning. Milestones can't be simply points on a line or red-letter days on a calendar. They've got to function in account management like "process controls" function in manufacturing.

In the old, precomputer days, when industrial machinery ran too hot or there was an operational malfunction somewhere on an assembly line, the whole line would often shut down until the problem could be identified and corrected. That prevented such disasters as overheated boilers turning into bombs, but it led to a lot of downtime and subsequent productivity losses. Today's computerized process controls are more sophisticated. They can pinpoint a problem much more quickly, making temperature or atmospheric adjustments while the line is still running. The feedback, in other words, is interactive—and the resulting cost savings can be great.

The interactive, quick adjustments made by process controls are an excellent model for account managers. Milestones are the checkpoints for those adjustments. And the aim, in account management no less than in manufacturing, is better *control* over your operation.

STRATEGY WORKSHOP 8: OBJECTIVES

In this workshop you'll operationalize your planning by breaking your Goals down into short-term Objectives. Accomplishing any account Goal will usually involve the attainment of several Objectives, and at the same time each individual Objective could contribute to the achievement of several Goals. For the purposes of this exercise, however, we'll ask you to focus on one Goal and one Objective. Our logic is an extension of the chunking principle. We suggest that you identify and plan for one "splinter" first. But we encourage you to use this single exercise as a model for further Objectives and for all your Goals.

Step 1. Select one Goal.

Of the Goals you identified in Strategy Workshop 5, select the one that you consider most important. It could be one of the "soft," value-centered Goals that relate to your customer's perception of your relationship, or it could be your Primary Revenue Target. Just be sure it accurately represents where your company wants to be with this customer one to three years from now. Write down the selected Goal in your notebook.

Step 2. Review your current situation.

Now look at today's reality, using as a guide the Situation Appraisal Summary that you put together in chapter 9. Take a few minutes to review the information in that document and to discuss how it relates to your stated Goal. You don't need to go into great detail. You're aiming for a "distance shot" of what lies ahead—or, more precisely, of the level of work that needs to be done to bridge the gap between reality and your end result. We recommend that you ask yourself particularly where you are most *strongly* positioned with regard to the Goal or Primary Revenue Target and where your position is *weakest*.

Step 3. How much can be accomplished this year?

Now look at the coming twelve months. Of the numerous tasks that have to be performed to reach the Goal, how many of them can be accomplished this year? Spend ten or fifteen minutes, as a team, in identifying and briefly describing the most important Objectives for that period. You may find a dozen, or only a couple, of these stepping-stones. Each Objective should be *measurable* (in terms of volume, revenue, and so on) and each one should be *realistic* (doable within the coming year).

Step 4. Select one Objective.

Now select the one Objective that the team believes should become the *first* stepping-stone toward your Goal. Resist the temptation to pick the Objective that is likely to pull in the quickest revenues. That *might* be the first one to tackle, but it might not. We urge you to focus on an Objective that is doable in the next *thirty to ninety days*. Write it down in your notebook, following this model:

We will (*sell, install, etc.*) (*amount*) of (*product or service*)
to (*portion of Large Account*) by (*date*).

Notice that your intention should be stated as an accomplishment
or an action: The words "sell" and "install" in the model are
examples of the "actionability" a good Objective requires. Remember too that the "amount" can be stated in revenue dollars,
units shipped, tonnage, or whatever measure matters to you. By
"portion of Large Account" we mean the specific department,
branch, or other entity that is going to purchase your product or
service.

Step 5. Identify the Corporate Results.

Even though you define Objectives, your customer still has to be
satisfied that they will help his or her bottom line. So check the
validity of this Objective by writing down, as specifically as you
can, the contribution that it will make to the Large Account, as
seen by the account's corporate management. Remember that a
Corporate Result has an impact on *profit* in one of three ways: it
(1) improves customers' sales to *their* customers; (2) increases
their productivity; or (3) lowers their operating costs. If your
chosen Objective doesn't affect one of these areas, it's not going to
bring you to your Goals.

Step 6. Establish Milestones.

Once you've defined the specific Objective you want to reach in
thirty to ninety days, get even more specific. Break down this
one- to three-month period into a series of Milestones. Recall that
a Milestone is a task or action that must be performed by a
scheduled date in order to move you toward the Objective.
Milestones include all the nitty-gritty operations of selling:
phone calls, meetings, information sessions, clearances, ap-
provals. You know your business and the types of things that have
to happen to put a given sale through. Itemize those tasks in this
step. Give them a schedule. And *assign* them to individuals or
teams. Not "Davison to be seen by May 12," but "Jen Ryan to see
Davison by May 12."

In allocating responsibility for reaching Milestones, keep one thing in mind. You can assign a *task* for a person to complete, but you can't really assign accountability. It's the people themselves who become accountable, because they see their own self-interest served by the performance of the task. To borrow a phrase that we use in *Strategic Selling*, people accomplish things—in and out of account management—because they feel that they'll "win" by doing so. Therefore, in assigning Milestone tasks, be sure that each person sees a personal "win" in the accomplishment of the Objective. If the win's not there, you can't expect the work.

You will probably find, as you think about this and your other Objectives, that closing the gap between today's reality and the dry ink on that September 15 contract may take more than just getting Jen to call on Davis and Tony to cover the bases with the finance chief. Most Objectives, like Goals, demand not just individual but corporate involvement—which means they require *program* support. We move now to that essential feature of corporate planning.

‖17‖

Closing the Gap

Once you've identified your priority Objectives, you need to determine what efforts your company must apply in order to accomplish them.

We distinguish between individual and company efforts. You already know how important we consider it for Objective-related tasks to be assigned to responsible individuals and for their progress toward those Objectives to be tracked. But individual (or account team) effort is seldom enough. To make things happen in Large Account planning, two distinct types of "extra" effort—effort that has *corporate* endorsement—must also be put into place.

These "extras" are programs designed to affect sales directly and programs that support the selling effort. The following diagram indicates why they're so important.

THE REALITY-OBJECTIVES GAP DEFINED

Consider the line we have labeled the momentum curve. This line represents the direction that your account development is most likely to take if you continue with *current* levels of effort. That effort may already be prodigious. Your planning team may be constantly in touch with the Large Account, and your salespeople may be pulling down record commissions. Nevertheless, in a dynamic, increasingly competitive atmosphere, "more of the

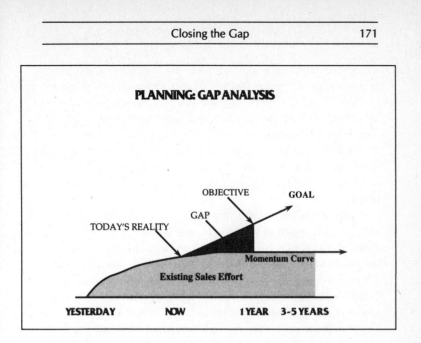

PLANNING: GAP ANALYSIS

OBJECTIVE GOAL

GAP

TODAY'S REALITY

Momentum Curve

Existing Sales Effort

YESTERDAY NOW 1 YEAR 3-5 YEARS

same" is inevitably a recipe for the kind of flat growth the curve illustrates.

One obvious reason is competition. As your competitors step up their efforts to secure business in your Large Accounts, you've got to do the same or fall behind. It's not comfortable, but it's reality: On a fast field, the merely good runner stumbles. Ask any manufacturer or any business that is still relying on "good products and services" while the competition is providing "extras" and "solutions."

A second reason "more of the same" is never enough is that both Objectives and Goals are, by definition, out of reach. If you could secure an Objective by continuing to do what you've been doing, it wouldn't be an Objective; it would be your inevitable tomorrow. As the diagram suggests, we don't believe in "inevitable" anythings. Objectives and Goals are "up and away" from today's reality; if your company exerts no more than today's efforts to reach them, they'll *always* be out of reach.

The dark shaded area above the momentum curve in the diagram expresses this. The straight line going from "today's reality" toward the Goal is a kind of "intention vector": It says how you'd like the next two or three years to look. Unless you've already achieved all your Objectives and Goals, there will inevitably be a gap between that vector and your momentum curve.

Here's the scary part. As time goes on, unless you increase your level of effort, that gap is bound to get wider. For one thing, you're likely to lose momentum relative to your competition—thus sending the bottom curve into a downward plunge that isn't even pictured in the graph. For another, failing to stretch for an improved position will push your Goals ever further out in front of you.

As the two-directional arrow to the right of the diagram suggests, it's important to identify the gap because that's where the value of planning is highest. You don't need intensive planning for your current efforts, because that work is already getting done. Planning for the far-distant future—far *beyond* your Goals—has little relation to near-term Objectives. But while you're *in* the gap, planning is crucial. Inertia will keep you stuck on the momentum curve, and only *increased* effort can help you "fill the gap." That increased effort must take the form of well-planned programs that complement what you're doing now.

CLOSING THE GAP: TWO TYPES OF PROGRAMS

We distinguish between two types of corporate programs designed to improve the effectiveness of your existing sales effort.

The first type is the *sales program*. We define a sales program as an activity or set of activities designed to produce sales revenue, but not necessarily tied to an individual sales Objective. Sales programs are part of the general account development process rather than targeted attacks on specific pieces of business.

Consider the following activities:

- Canvassing a division of your Large Account for new prospects.
- Generating leads through a direct mail campaign.
- Including in-product questionnaires to gauge customer satisfaction and responsiveness.
- Implementing an "executive call" program between managers in your Large Account and your company.

- Conducting needs surveys of current accounts.
- Conducting liability analyses.
- Touring customer plants or other operations.

In all of these activities, and in many others, the direct intent is to generate sales revenue. But companies that implement such sales programs can't say precisely where the money will come from. When you send out thousands of customer reply cards, you don't know which returns will turn into real prospects. When you send your operations vice president to call on a Large Account's CEO, you're not aiming for just one piece of business. Such programs are meant to secure sales growth and continuity over time, not to get approval for individual contracts.

The second type of program is even further removed from individual sales. A *support program* is an activity or set of activities that sustains or assists the selling effort but that does *not* directly generate sales revenue. Here we mean all those "backup" and "follow-up" programs that your company does to ensure customer satisfaction, but that don't figure into quotas or commissions. Some examples:

- Customer training programs.
- The installation or upgrading of equipment.
- Maintenance and "protective maintenance" calls by your service personnel.
- Repair calls.
- Extended warranty programs.
- The installation of customer-service 800 lines.

In such support programs, the revenue payoff is not always clear. They might be likened to "damage control" or "operating feedback" mechanisms designed to measure, and adjust, the existing sales effort. Many support programs don't even involve sales personnel: They're often implemented by engineers or customer service people, or by outside consultants. So their connection to individual pieces of business—the Model E19 calibrator placement, the Jeffries contract—can sometimes seem pretty distant.

Recall too the types of support that we mentioned in the chapter on the buy-sell hierarchy: the provision of such supposedly "nonbusiness" solutions as Kimberly-Clark's Executive

Exchange program or the loan of a negotiator for a customer's labor problems. Only in a very indirect manner do such programs support the selling effort; certainly their impact on individual sales is not obvious.

This does *not* mean they're unimportant.

On the contrary. The best-managed Large Account programs—the ones that are as dynamic as their environment and that most effectively close the gap between the momentum curve and desired Goals—spend a *great* deal of time supporting the sales effort, directly and indirectly, even where the immediate payoff is not obvious.

Such extra effort may seem peripheral to account management. It's not. In a real sense, truly managing your Large Accounts today *means* implementing sales and support programs that don't hook up to single sales Objectives. *Not* implementing such programs means losing out to the companies that do.

"WE CAN'T AFFORD IT"

We hear this reaction all the time. "We're already stretched too far on product development." "CEOs have got better things to do than schmooze customers." "Only huge corporations can afford the kind of programs you're talking about." And, most commonly, "We'd *like* to put all these marginal things in place, but we're stretched thin." Bottom line: We lack the budget and the time.

It's true that sales and support programs put money and time pressure on a company's resources. But thinking of this pressure as merely negative—or, in the worst-case scenario, as intolerable—is extremely shortsighted strategically. It's also, logistically speaking, not quite accurate. The planning and implementation of support programs doesn't necessarily mean *more* money or *more* work. It means the intelligent *reallocation* of funds and efforts so that you get more bang for the buck.

Seldom does the simple lack of resources inhibit support programs. Usually the problem is that *too many resources are being devoted to dead-end, low-potential business.* Free up those resources by Stop Investment, and you'll be amazed at how many programs are suddenly within the budget.

The money excuse is self-defeating in another way too. It

betrays the all-too-common notion that the "selling arm" is a kind of bionic cat's paw, unrelated to the corporate body and needing no support from the nerve center. In today's climate, that idea can be disastrous. You've got to *integrate* the "business side" with the "selling side," for the simple reason that each will die without the other. Gap-closing programs foster that integration.

In our discussion of the buy-sell hierarchy, we said that moving up means fighting your competition every step of the way. And we mentioned a subtle kind of "bracket creep" that occurs as you grapple for new footholds: Today's "extras" are constantly turning into tomorrow's "givens," as the "minimum acceptable" curve spirals upward. Among these extras are the sales and support programs we're recommending. They're not really extras anymore; they've become part of every serious player's entry fee. If they're not part of your planning to close the reality-Objectives gap, you're going to fall into that gap, great selling aside.

Can you afford to support your accounts with such "peripheral" programs? The question should be "Can you afford *not* to?"

STRATEGY WORKSHOP 9: CLOSING THE GAP

Having committed individual and team efforts to accomplishing your Objectives, you're now going to identify corporate sales and support programs to ensure that those efforts bear fruit. To help you develop ideas, we'll give you the same series of questions the LAMP clients use in their "Closing the Gap" workshops. In working from these questions, remember that a *sales* program is designed to generate sales, although it's not limited to a specific sales objective. A *support* program assists the sales effort; it's often run by non-sales people in your organization.

A general guideline. Consider not only the business relationship you've established but your business, and the Large Account's business, in general. You should be looking for *whatever you do well* that can impact positively, in whatever way, on the customer's concerns.

Step 1. Solving the Customer's Problems.

Concentrate first on programs you might put into place that can address any of your Large Account's problems. We do mean "any." The programs don't have to be related to individual sales; they don't even have to connect to the business you do with the account. For example, ask:

- What actions can we take to remedy a customer's *service* problem? Either our service to the customer, or his or her service to somebody else.
- What can we do to solve a customer's *product* problems? Again, this means either the products we sell to the customer, or those that he or she sells customers.
- The last time we solved a problem for this customer, how did we do it? The last time our competition solved a problem for this customer, how did they do it?
- Is there a problem on this customer's horizon that a program of ours might head off? What activities might we engage in that could help us "save" the customer before he or she's in trouble?

Step 2. Addressing the customer's top-level issues.

Now look at possible Corporate Results that you could provide to this Large Account. Remembering that long-term account management rests on satisfying top management concerns, ask:

- What activities could we pursue to position us higher up the buy-sell relational hierarchy?
- How can we help this account increase *sales revenue* from its own accounts?
- How can we improve the account's own *productivity*?
- Can we do something to help reduce its *costs*?
- What can we do to help this customer untangle an *internal* problem?
- Most important of all, what actions can we undertake that will have a positive impact on the customer's *profit*?

Step 3. Broadening our scope.

Look at areas of potential activity that would broaden the scope of your "investment" in this field of play or this Large Account. Define programs that might target business you have overlooked. Ask:

- What sales and marketing approaches could we try that we haven't tried before?
- What are we doing with other accounts that we haven't considered doing here?
- Are there overlooked business Opportunities here? What programs would altering the field of play or the "what" of our Charter Statement suggest?
- What other locations or business units of this Large Account have problems that we might address?

Step 4. Confronting threats.

Think defensively for a few minutes. You may feel yourself to be on the offensive with this account at this time. But suppose you were being pushed into a corner. What extra effort would you then begin to consider? Ask:

- If our job(s) depended on a 50 percent increase in revenues this year from this account, what programs would we come up with?
- What actions might our major competitor take to unseat us in this account? Are any of those actions applicable to our situation; that is, do they suggest programs we could put in place?
- If we were about to lose the account, what defense would we take? If it was a choice of do or die, what would the extra effort be?

Step 5. Working with megabucks.

To counter the all-too-common objection that the budget won't allow innovation, pretend there's no such thing as a budget. Ask:

- If a company like Mitsubishi, General Motors, or Citicorp wanted to own this account, what programs would *it* put into place?
- What would we do with a blank-check program development fund?

- In an ideal world, with no resource limitation, what activities would we pursue for this account?

Yes, these final three questions are "off the wall." But we've found that they're also useful in getting account teams to entertain innovation—to think beyond the old Don't-buck-the-bucks mentality that can spell defeat in the most hard-working of organizations.

Along with innovation, however, you also need a strong dash of realism. We're going to bring those two necessary qualities together now, as you set assignments and schedules for the best of the programs you've just generated, as part of a four-quarter Action Plan.

‖18‖

Putting It All Together

STAGE THREE:

YOUR ACTION PLAN

Throughout this program, you've been gathering and then distilling information to improve your strategic position with your
Large Account. At the end of part II, you pulled the available
information together into a Situation Appraisal Summary. At the
end of part III, working with the principles of Goals and time
investment, you created a Draft Strategy for your targeted account. Now, using the principles of Objectives and Milestones,
you're going to pull the information together one more time,
creating a four-quarter Action Plan that gives the who, what, and
when of your strategy.

You won't be generating new information in this workshop,
but that doesn't mean it's a copying exercise. The plan you'll
create here is a Large Account "white paper" that will guide your
company's actions for the next twelve months. It will require an
hour or more to create it. It's crucial that all team members
participate in constructing it, that they review and endorse it,
and that the individuals responsible for performing specific actions recognize and accept their accountability.

STRATEGY WORKSHOP 10: ACTION PLAN

Begin by opening your notebook flat, so that you're looking at two
new facing pages. Across the top of these pages write the title

"Goal Action Plan" and the following identifying information: the name of the Large Account or portion of that account you're targeting, today's date, your single most significant Goal, and your Primary Revenue Target.

In this workshop you'll construct an Action Plan designed specifically to accomplish just one Goal. We recommend that you use this as a model to construct separate Goal Action Plans for the other major Goals you've identified. When you bring all these Goal Action Plans together, they'll comprise a complete Account Action Plan.

When you write in your Primary Revenue Target, we suggest writing down the total figures, then breaking it down into "pieces" to be achieved over the next four quarters. But don't just divide the total Primary Revenue Target figure into four equal chunks. Consider the revenue history you've had with this account, the seasonal ebb and flow in your industry, and your revenue projections for this field of play at this time; then make your quarterly Primary Revenue Target estimates.

After you've written in this basic information, divide the Action Plan into six columns—three to each open page. At the top of the far-left column, write the heading "Objectives," and in the *same* column about halfway down the page, write another heading, "Programs." At the top of the second column, write the heading "Current Quarter, FY 19____," and fill in the relevant fiscal year. Label the third, fourth, and fifth columns appropriately for the upcoming three quarters: For example, if it's now the third quarter of 1991, the fifth column in your chart would be labeled "Second Quarter, FY 1992." Finally, label the sixth column "Comments" and divide the entire two-page chart into ten or twelve horizontal rows. When you're finished, your notebook should look something like the chart on pages 182 and 183.

Step 1. Identify your Objectives.

In the Strategy Workshop on Objectives in chapter 16, your team identified measurable, realistic Objectives for the coming twelve months that could get you toward your highest priority Goal.

Select the six or seven most important of those Objectives and write them down in the left-hand column of the chart. For each Objective, you should identify the *product* (or *service*) you will sell, install, deliver, and so on; the amount of *revenue* ($) that will be realized; and the expected *date* by which the Objective will be realized. Remember that each of these chosen Objectives should bring you closer to your priority Goal.

In the Objectives workshop, although we insisted that you state the amount of product to be delivered, we said that you could state it in any measure that made sense to you: dollars, units, tonnage. Because you're now implementing a Goal Action Plan that is linked directly to account revenue, you should translate each measure into dollars—even if the translation is a rough estimate. Having each Objective defined in terms of expected dollar revenues will make it easier for you, as you periodically review this plan, to measure the distance between where you are at any given moment and your Primary Revenue Target.

Step 2. Identify sales and support programs.

Now turn to the programs that you generated in the chapter 17 workshop on Closing the Gap. In the left-hand column of the chart, write in the four or five most significant ones under the heading "Programs." By "significant" we mean those programs that are likely to have a long-term impact on a number of Objectives. You'll recall that a good Gap-closing program isn't tied in with only one Objective: It's not designed to "make the Rogers sale" or "get the model E19 calibrators in place." Because they enhance the business relationship, programs usually impact on several sales. The ideal line of impact is from a program *through* several Objectives, to your Goal.

Step 3. Set Milestones.

Now comes the most difficult and yet most rewarding part of account planning. For each of the Objectives that you have written in, establish Milestones for those tasks that must be accom-

GOAL ACTION PLAN   Goal:

Objectives	Current Quarter FY 19__	____ Quarter FY 19__
Programs		

Primary Revenue Target _____

Q1 _____   Q2 _____   Q3 _____   Q4 _____

_____ Quarter FY 19__	_____ Quarter FY 19__	Comments

plished if the Objective is to be reached on time, and note the deadline dates for those tasks in the appropriate columns of the chart: work that has to get done this quarter goes in column 2, next quarter's work goes in column 3, and so on. For each Milestone that you write in, you should clearly indicate three things: *what* has to happen, the *date* it has to happen by, and the *person* responsible for making it happen.

You've already done this once before, in the Strategy Workshop in chapter 16. But there you worked with an Objective that was only three months away, and the Milestones schedule was correspondingly short. Here you're plotting a course of actions for a full year, to secure not only this quarter's Objectives but also those that are still months away. You've broken the chart up into quarterly columns to make this scheduling easier.

You may not need all four columns for every one of your targeted Objectives. For example, if the date for accomplishing Objective 3 is only two months away, you'll schedule Milestones for that Objective in the second column only. If Objective 5 is supposed to happen within eight months, you'll have Milestones in columns 2, 3, and 4. In either case, some of the columns may remain blank.

On the other hand, you may find that this sample chart is too limited to hold your entire schedule. The Objective that is two months away may involve four different Milestones, and there's no space to fit them in on the chart. If that's the case, modify this chart so it corresponds to your Objectives, your Large Account, your business. Our chart is a model. *Don't* attempt to modify your Goal or Objectives to fit the chart. If you need more detail— if a month-by-month schedule makes more sense, for example— then adjust your Goal Action Plan accordingly.

One more proviso. Don't feel you have to fill in all the blanks. You're not trying simply to turn white space black, but to define those individual activities that have to happen by specified dates to make your Objectives, and your Goal, a reality. We always feel it's better to write in *more* specifics rather than less, but you know your own need for detail. If you find yourself making up tasks because "column 2, line 3 is blank," you're playing connect-the-dots. That isn't planning.

Step 4. Schedule your programs.

Now do the same thing for sales and support programs that you just did for Objectives. Using our quarter-by-quarter model, or whatever schedule makes sense in your business, define who has to do what, and by when, to get the programs in place and up to speed.

Doing this for programs is a little different from doing it for Objectives, because few programs have "close dates" per se: They're more flexible, and ongoing, than sales Objectives. Nevertheless, they still involve planning, and thus the implementation of specific activities that individuals have to do by certain dates. So they too have to be scheduled and tracked. A partially filled-in plan follows this page.

Step 5. Get sign-off.

Account strategy can work only if *all* those affected by the strategy buy in to its basic propositions. To ensure that your Action Plan works the way you want it to, you need "sign-off" from three distinct groups of people:

• The *account team* devising the plan. Obvious enough, but not always done. *Everyone* who works on this Goal Action Plan should review and endorse the final version. This is especially, though not exclusively, important for the people who are responsible for implementing Milestones. You might have each of these people initial the relevant column to certify his or her accountability, or you can use the "Comments" column for that purpose.

• Your company *management*. Again obvious, but very seldom done. Because Large Accounts are the driving force of your business, your top management has got to know how they're being handled. Ideally, your top managers should be working members of your Large Account management teams themselves. Failing that, their *minimum* commitment should be to read and approve your Action Plan. If they can't, or won't, then you're probably kidding yourself about getting the corporate support that you need to make the plan work. That's a strong

GOAL ACTION PLAN

Goal: More reliable QC with our unified systems approach

Objectives	Current Quarter FY 19___	_____ Quarter FY 19___
Place ten E19s		June 15 Jess's group
Research analysis of process controls	March 30: Harry meet w/Mary Hurley	May 25: MH to deliver specs to Harry
Install pilot run QC program,		April 10: Demo to Rackham Jess
jointly w/Reffen		June 6: Spec Sheet, answer Finance questions Harry
Programs		
User group implementation	March 30: Harry invite Mary Hurley	
Mailing to all units re E19s	March 25: Get org. list. Alice.	May 20: list to printer. Alice
Service checking of E19s		June 15: Check service specs on signing. Jess

_____ Quarter FY 19__	_____ Quarter FY 19__	Comments
August 1-4: First run. Jess coordinate		
July 15: Meeting w/R&D Unit. Jess, Harry	October 10: Installation (Reffen)	Installation to be checked at 30-day intervals ⟶
August 12: Finance Sign-off. Harry	November 15: 1st check December 15: 2nd check (Reffen)	
	October 25: User meeting, Chicago. Harry, Jen	
August 1: Mailing Alice	October 1: Follow-up Alice, Jim	
Gerry 1st check: July 15 2nd check: August 15 3rd check: September 15	4th: October 15 5th: November 15 6th: December 15 Gerry	

statement, we realize; the experience of *dozens* of companies proves its validity.

• Key Players in the *Large Account*. Not obvious at all, and almost never done—but just as essential as getting your own management to buy-in. We don't mean you should ask the account's decision makers to initial every one of your Milestones. But they should understand in general terms what you're about, and specifically they should be able to endorse your Goal, your Objectives, and your sales and support programs. If you don't have this kind of client buy-in, you're cutting yourself off from a different kind of corporate support—support that's just as critical as support from your own management.

YOUR TEAM—AND THEIRS

If you're uncomfortable with this idea, it may be because the Goals you have set with this account are not as consistent with a "win-win" relationship as your team supposes—or because your current position with the account is weaker than you imagined. If that's the case, reexamine your position to see if correcting the reasons for your discomfort would involve a redefinition of your Goals. When you are *positioned effectively* at an account, you should have *no hesitancy in sharing with the firm's decision makers the substance of your plans*.

The presentation of account plans to your Large Account is not only an important feature of "win-win" business. It's also a good reality check against blue-sky thinking. If Key Players at your Large Account can't or won't acknowledge the *mutual* advantages of your Goals, Objectives, and programs, you cannot build a partnership upon them.

But that's a negative way of putting it. You can also see it positively. When your Large Account *does* buy in to the Goals and Objectives that you've targeted, you begin to see each other as part of the same, not rival, teams. And the whole strategy runs that much more smoothly. It's as if you have a "companion general" across the field, providing you information you could not get on your own. Pragmatics again: You make the Large Account part of your planning process not because it's a "nice" thing to do, but because it makes for better business.

In a sense this is a microversion of a broader point we have made throughout the book. Good Large Account management isn't magic. It's based on the principle that, when people believe you have their interests as well as your own at heart, they'll fight to keep doing business with you. If they don't believe that, they'll run like hell to avoid you.

The lesson, once again, is "thinking with the customer's mind." It includes sharing what's in *your* mind regarding the account. It's like putting your cards faceup on the table, to show how you would like to play the game. Not as exciting as close-to-the-vest, six-wild-cards poker, maybe. But a lot more reliable.

YOUR ACCOUNT ACTION PLAN

We've advised you to draw up an Action Plan that is focused on a single account Goal. The logic here is to avoid a common error in developing your strategy Goals: the belief that all your individual sales Objectives, as long as you pursue them intelligently, eventually impact on all of your Goals. Occasionally you do find this kind of multiple impact, but more often than not it's a phantom. The best strategies we've observed over the years make it clear— in a visible, written plan—how individual Objectives tie in to *specific* long-range Goals. Any "spillover" of benefits into other Goals should be taken as a plus, *not* a given.

The reason is that, in expecting a given Objective to further two or three or ten Goals, you lose the focus of intent that enabled you to draft a sharply defined Goal in the first place. When that happens, the Objective can become an end in itself, as you forget what your planning was supposed to accomplish. Vagueness sets in, you work on the Objective without knowing why, and your strategy becomes an exercise without a purpose.

But the improvement of your overall account position is the result of having met several Goals. For this reason, the Goal Action Plan you've just devised, while it's clear and distinct in itself, must also be seen as part of a larger whole. That larger whole, your Account Action Plan, includes the entire "portfolio" of Goal Action Plans that your team devises for a given Large Account. We recommend that you make Goal Action Plans for at least your two or three other major Goals and that you bring them together, physically, into a portfolio. This will enable you both to distinguish between your various account Goals and to identify, in a concise fashion, what they have in common.

The Account Action Plan that thus results will map out, clearly and accessibly, a way of doing business with this Large Account over the next nine to twelve months. We suggest that you operate on this plan for three months and then subject it to a ninety-day review. The next chapter describes how to perform such a review.

PART V

Looking Back
—and Ahead

||19||

The Ninety-Day
Review

The LAMP programs that we introduce to our corporate clients involve three distinct phases of implementation: a preprogram phase of fact-gathering and account analysis, the program proper, and a ninety-day follow-up workshop. The research that we asked you to do in chapter 4 corresponds to LAMP's preprogram phase. The work that you did in parts II through IV of the book corresponds to the program proper. We're now going to introduce you to the review analysis that our clients do in the follow-up workshop.

This third phase is not an "add on." It's a critical component of LAMP strategy for the simple reason that the world is always changing. The Action Plan you've just devised for your Large Account depicts what you *intend* to have happen over the next twelve months. Any number of internal and external imponderables could impact on what actually *does* happen. In only the past several months, for example, anyone doing business internationally has had to begin rethinking his or her strategy to account for a 50 percent rise in oil prices *and* the unification of the two Germanies—events that were entirely unpredictable a few years ago, yet that have tremendous significance for businesses around the globe.

The moral is simple. After designing an Action Plan, you must pause along the way from time to time, to confirm that the signposts you've laid out are still pointing you in the right direction.

We encourage such a reassessment of your position at approximately the ninety-day mark, or one fiscal quarter into the strategy. This checkpoint is chosen not arbitrarily, but from trial and error. We've found it takes at least two or three months for planning to begin to bear fruit; by four or five months down the line, it may already be too late to make corrections.

So, if you've been using our workshops all along to set strategy for a targeted Large Account, you should be ready to apply the lessons of this review chapter about ninety days after completing your Action Plan. This doesn't mean you should put the book down and dust it off three months from now. We recommend, on the contrary, that you do the following:

- Read through this chapter quickly now, to get a sense of what you'll be looking for when it comes time to review your Action Plan.
- Read the final chapter as well. It proposes a rethinking of corporate philosophy that has a direct effect on account management. Understanding what we mean by "reintegrating" the selling function can profoundly influence the process of review *and* the value of your current Action Plan.

Once you've done that, set a date for the review workshop and get commitment from everyone who needs to be there. That includes not only your account team members but also sales and general management in your company and key players in the targeted Large Account. The same guidelines we laid out in chapter 3 for the Strategy Workshops apply just as clearly to this one. The better the information and the greater the commitment, the better the review.

STRATEGY WORKSHOP 11:
NINETY-DAY REVIEW

In this review workshop, you will measure the progress you have made against your Action Plan, problem-solve for glitches in your strategy, revise your Goals and Objectives where necessary, and set new actions in the light of what has happened.

Step 1. Revisit the Charter Statement.

The Charter Statement your team devised for this Large Account identified three things: the field of play within the account, what products or services you sold there, and the value added to the customer's business as a result. Look again at those three pieces. In the light of what has occurred in the past ninety days, ask:

• Is this *field of play* still appropriate? Did we correctly define the scope of our operations in this account, and does that definition still apply? Have we been trying to reach too broad a portion of the target company—trying to sell to too many people, departments, divisions, or other business units? Or, on the other hand, have we overlooked opportunities in the account by defining our field of play too narrowly?

• Are we selling the *optimal* range of our products or services? Not the broadest possible range, but the best one. Are our offerings proving to be too wide for what this customer really needs? Too narrow? What products or services might we reasonably withdraw from consideration without sacrificing our effectiveness in the account? What products or services might we add?

• What *value* have we added to this customer's business by focusing on this field of play? Are we truly providing solutions to the account's business problems, or are we still in a "cramming product" mode? Can we clearly define the Corporate Results that this customer has realized as a result of doing business with us? Finally, in the three months since we implemented our Action Plan, have we moved up or down the business relationship hierarchy? If we haven't moved up, why not? If we're down, what are the reasons for the slippage?

Once you've discussed these questions, decide as a team whether the Charter Statement you established three months ago still makes sense, or whether it has to be rewritten against today's reality.

Step 2. Define your accomplishments.

In any ninety-day period, some things are going to go right and others wrong. In this step, define what's been going right: the major accomplishments of your Action Plan strategy. Focus on three separate types of accomplishments:

• *Sales victories*. That is, individual Objectives achieved (on or before schedule), or any other product or service packages placed with this Large Account. Define these precisely, as you always define Objectives: "We sold them the E19 calibrators we had planned to" or "We placed twelve, rather than the anticipated ten, calibrators." For each sales "victory," note the revenue brought in and the close date. Compare these figures to the "intended" figures that you wrote down in your Action Plan.

• *Sales and support programs*. Write down those programs that you have successfully put in place, whether or not they have resulted in identifiable revenue. How do these "program victories" tie in to the four or five intended programs that you identified on your Action Plan? What specific *progress* do you see in the account for each of the programs that have been put into place? For programs that are still in the development stage, write down the progress that your team sees toward their implementation. You can't be as revenue-oriented here as you can with your product and service victories, but you can be specific: "Karen Jensen made first executive call on their finance vice president." "Chicago direct-mail campaign now in progress."

• *Other accomplishments*. You define them. We encourage you to be inclusive rather than limiting, provided that each identified accomplishment is clearly moving your account team ahead in its long-term strategy. Example: Taking an executive from the Large Account to lunch might well be a significant strategy accomplishment, but *only* if that person is a Key Player for this field of play and with regard to your business, and only if the results of that meeting included greater commitment from the client, and thus improved position for you.

A brief clarification regarding "commitment." In our second book, *Conceptual Selling*, we emphasized the importance of *mutual* commitment between buyer and seller. It's never enough, we pointed out, for a customer merely to "think about" the terms of a business relationship while the seller commits real time and real resources into moving that relationship forward. Yes, the seller may have to bear the weight at the outset, but if I've met with key players from the Betco Group three times and they *say* they're interested in working with my company, but the only commitment I can get out of them is a vague "Let's talk again soon," we may be wasting each other's time. It may be time not for Focus but for Stop Investment.

Commitment in a business relationship means commitment to *concrete, scheduled actions.* These may range from merely setting up the next appointment, to giving detailed responses to proposal specs, to the actual signing of an agreement between your firms. But the customer must demonstrate interest in partnering with you by making incremental investments of *his* or *her* resources as the negotiating process between you moves forward.

As you enter your ninety-day review, use this understanding as a check on your progress. What specifically has this customer done in the past ninety days to indicate an increasing level of interest in the relationship? What has it cost *his* or *her* company in terms of time and resources? If the investment is all on your side, it's not a partnership. And the great lunch you had with this customer's CEO may not have been a "victory" at all.

Step 3. Identify your problems.

Now look at the things that have gone wrong. Investigate the following problem areas:

• *Lost sales.* Look both at sales that have been lost to the competition and at opportunities that might have been developed in this Large Account, but that neither you nor your competition has capitalized on. For each piece of lost or undeveloped revenue, the team should say *why* it was lost: "We're not well enough positioned with their operations people." "The other side's got a better service record." "Their people are intimidated by our technology." Discuss what changes might be made in your strategy to prevent similar losses in the future. Obviously the presence of Large Account people here can be especially valuable; no one will know better than they do why you lost a particular piece of their business.

• *Program/resources issues*. What internal program and resources issues must still be resolved in order to put your plan into operation? Are budget constraints—perceived or real ones—making it difficult for your team to close the gap? Do you have to do more aggressive internal selling to free up the funds needed to manage this account? How do your company's top managers see your Action Plan? Are they committed to its implementation? Or must they still be convinced that it's worth the investment? Compare the issues you identify here with the sales losses you've just listed: Could any of those losses have been prevented by a fuller resource commitment? What are the views of people in the Large Account itself regarding the connection between these programs and your level of business?

• *Other obstacles*. What other obstacles stand in the way of an effective implementation of your Action Plan? List *anything* that has hindered your progress, no matter how "trivial." Look especially for two common types of obstacles: *people* in your own company or in the account organization who may lack full commitment to your plan, and areas where you lack *information* regarding this Large Account and your business's place in it. Review the areas of account information that you addressed in chapter 4. Is the information you discovered there still valid? Any areas where you have unclear or incomplete information are by definition obstacles to an Action Plan.

• *"Off-line" areas*. Since you laid out the Action Plan, have there been any sales Objectives, sales or support programs, or other significant resources allocated to this account that have proved "off line" or even against the strategy plan? Strategy by definition brings you closer to a sound long-term relationship. What activities have you been performing that aren't doing that? They may be candidates for a Stop Investment. If your team can identify any activities that aren't clearly bringing you closer to your Goals, write them down, explain *why* they're failing to live up to their promise, and consider dropping them from your Action Plan.

Step 4. Reassess your Opportunities.

In the Draft Strategy you devised in chapter 14, you identified your four best Opportunities. Remembering that an Opportunity exists *in the account*, revisit those four best choices now, adjusting and redefining where necessary.

• For each of the four best Opportunities, can you still define the *reason* it's valid? Has anything happened in the past ninety days to make you reconsider your initial evaluation? If an Opportunity is still worth going after, your team should be able to explain why.

• Does each Opportunity still relate to your Goals? Look at each of the four Opportunities in turn. Can you identify *at least* one strategic Goal that the pursuit of this Opportunity will further? If not, should you drop this Opportunity in favor of another one? Or do your Goals themselves need redefining?

• Restate the four best Opportunities, based on the reassessment you've just performed and on changed conditions. They may be the same four you started out with three months ago, or you may have to redirect your actions and resources.

• Restate the Goals you established in your Draft Strategy. Again, they may be unchanged, or you may have to redefine them in the light of current reality.

• Finally, when you've reset your Opportunities and your Goals, identify *at least one* sales Objective that should be pursued to get you to each Goal. Compare these Objectives with the seven Objectives you laid out in the Action Plan. Should any be dropped? Added? Rewritten?

Step 5. Summarize.

Now pull together all you've looked at in this workshop, and focus on the most important discoveries. As a way of distilling out the critical factors, we recommend that you draw a three-column chart in your notebook. Label the chart "Ninety-Day Review." Head the left-hand column "Five Critical Facts," the middle column "Opportunity or Threat," and the right-hand column

"Implications for Strategy." Divide the space under the columns into five rows. Then list the five facts you've uncovered in this review that your team feels are most critical to the retooling of your strategy. Decide whether they're primarily threats or primarily opportunities (they could, of course, be both), and define what implications they have for your strategy.

By "most critical" we mean what *you* consider critical, no matter what the LAMP principle or area involved. By "threats or opportunities," we mean: Is it a threat or an opportunity to your *current* strategy, as laid out in the working Action Plan? By "implications," we mean *action* implications: What should you continue doing, start doing, or stop doing to meet the threat or the opportunity of this fact?

Step 6. Reset the Action Plan.

Now put the ninety-day review you've just done and the original Action Plan side by side. Almost certainly modifications will be in order. We suggest that you make these changes not by penciling in corrections but by resetting the entire Action Plan, so that it "begins" again, with today's date as the starting line. The original first column, listing your Objectives and programs, may change because some of them have already been accomplished and others need redefinition in order to work. The original second column will drop out of view, because the schedule there is already in the past. Everything else (except the "Comments" column) will move ninety days to the left: the original third column will become the new second column, the fourth will become the third, the fifth will become the fourth, and you'll draw up an entirely new fifth column. Then you'll rewrite the entire plan, keeping in mind not only this shift but also the five "implications" that your team has just identified.

Perhaps the most critical feature of this resetting process is adjusting the action schedule based on changing events and on the accountability that has (or has not) been established. We're not Pollyannas about this. We know very well that, after ninety days, some tasks are going to be done with ribbons and bows and some are going to look like a teenager's closet. One of the most important benefits of regular review is to find out who's on board and who's asleep at the wheel—and to reappoint and reschedule the tasks accordingly.

In the example we provided back in chapter 16, Tony Mustelli was assigned to present a contract for legal review by August 5. If the ninety-day review comes up on September 1 and that task hasn't yet been done, you know the entire Action Plan has to be rescheduled, and the team has got to understand the reason why the August 5 deadline was not met.

This doesn't necessarily mean blasting Tony. He may have very good reasons why the deadline wasn't met, and those reasons can provide valuable information for the realistic resetting of the schedule. But you won't *get* such information, in most cases, until you ask—which is precisely why regular review is essential to strategy. Regular review—whether it happens every ninety days or once a week—*institutionalizes the asking of relevant questions*, so that nobody on your team has to labor under the delusion that piece 14 of the plan is working when it's not.

Two other benefits inherent in regular review point to the ongoing, dynamic nature of LAMP analysis.

One is that such review provides *documented feedback* on how effectively a plan is working and where it's not. As we pointed out in the introduction, most corporate account "plans" don't even try to do that: They're collections of old statistics and yesterday's news. A dynamic, constantly reassessed Action Plan lets you know *while you can still do something about it* where it's working and where it needs retooling. And it does this in black and white, with everybody's sign-off.

The other is that, unlike most account "plans," the LAMP review process that we're suggesting here of necessity involves your top management in the resetting, as well as the original design, of account strategy. You know that we consider this essential to the effective management of Large Accounts in the 1990s. We're going to tie up this book by explaining why.

‖20‖

An Immodest Proposal: Straight Talk for Senior Managers

In an old movie about the Plains Indians, there is a scene in which a group of tribal elders convene to discuss the wisdom of breaking camp. They have lived on the shore of the same lake for three years, delighting in its quiet beauty and clean water. But the buffalo on which the tribe depends for food have begun to migrate west; as a result, feeding the people has become problematic. The elders know they must follow the buffalo eventually. But how soon?

For several minutes the chiefs debate the alternatives, some favoring an immediate move, others a fourth winter along the lake and a spring departure. Then one of them addresses a pair of young hunters, sitting respectfully across the council fire. What do they think? Can the remaining buffalo feed the people until the spring?

Politely but firmly, the young men answer no. If the tribe stays until the snows have come and gone, the animals will have wandered too far. During the spring pursuit, food will be scarce. The people will surely be hungry, and some will die.

After hearing the young men's comments, the chiefs decide. "The hunters know the buffalo best. If they say to follow them now, we must do so." So the tents are struck, the horses are packed—and the tribe survives.

What, you may reasonably ask, does this have to do with business?

The answer is that, in following the hunters' advice to move the camp, the elders were observing two principles of organizational management that are just as relevant to today's complex corporations as they were to nineteenth-century Indian tribes.

First, if you expect to survive as an organization, you've got to ensure the availability of basic resources.

Second, in securing those resources, it's reasonable to ask for the input of resource experts.

These principles are only common sense. Unfortunately for many modern businesses, however, their "chiefs" don't share the Indians' managerial savvy. In fact, in today's corporate environment, it is rare to the point of laughability for managers to take such basic axioms to heart. In all but the most superbly managed firms, company "elders" commonly ignore the "food supply" while condescending to the overworked "hunters" who bring it in.

"SILVER-TONGUED DEVIL STRIKES AGAIN"

The "food supply" of any modern corporation is the revenue that is generated by its major accounts. You could probably find an MBA student at Harvard or Stanford to "disprove" this fact, showing that it's really "creative accounting," just-in-time inventory control, or some other hot new B-schoolism that keeps the corporation "nimble" and productive. Yet to anybody *in* business, that's profspeak gibberish. One thing and one thing only keeps you running: the income from the products and services you sell your customers. If that income isn't your "buffalo," Adam Smith isn't dead.

If the "food" of the corporation is sales revenue, it follows that a company's "hunters" are its sales professionals: From the field representative out "foraging" for leads, to the account manager who sets the quotas and sweats the numbers, to the service people who follow up on customer problems, it's people in the sales and sales support segments of your business that ensure the reliability of your most essential resource. It's no exaggeration to say that sales forces provide the life blood of all corporate relationships.

If most senior managers recognized this, they would include the sales force not only in "delivering the goods" but in the long-term, strategic management of the *business* itself. They'd be asking, on a regular basis, not just "Where's the beef?" but also "Where do you think we should be moving?" In a business that was run on common sense, the chiefs and the hunters would regularly "powwow" together, and what the hunters said would be taken *very* seriously.

In very few businesses does this happen. Far from focusing on the value that good salespeople bring their firms, senior managers tend to focus on the most negative aspects of the hunter-seller analogy, treating their sales professionals as little more than hired guns—expendable pawns in a dog-eat-dog game.

The difference in perspective is subtle but crucial. When you see your salespeople as resource providers, you can accept the end result as being the development of better business and see the customer as a potential partner in that development. But if you take the "hunter" analogy in its most restrictive sense, the sales professional becomes someone who shoots things down, and the customer becomes the target of aggression.

This latter view of the seller as customer-slayer is as incompatible with healthy business as it is old-fashioned. You can't last five minutes today by treating your customers as if they were buffalo. Yet the myth persists. To much of the public, the very term "salesperson" still connotes Sam Slick: the silver-tongued devil who can talk the ears off a brass monkey and who cares as much about meeting his customers' needs as a barracuda cares what it has for lunch. According to the conventional wisdom, salespeople subscribe to a very simple canon: "Promise the moon if you have to. Just *make the sale*."

Corporate managers often add to this negative opinion an equally negative complaint of their own. Gung-ho salespeople, they say, undermine not only their own credibility but that of their firms as well by making promises they know cannot be kept. In these managers' view, the supposed Sam Slick credo reads "Make the sale no matter what it costs your company."

What these frustrated managers seldom recognize, and *never* admit, is that the silver-tongued devil they complain about is a

Frankenstein monster they themselves have created. They've done so by giving their salespeople two absolutely contradictory sets of instructions.

MIXED MESSAGES

The first message that salespeople get is an agreeable one: "Stay close to the customer. We want solid, mutually beneficial relationships with our accounts. We want you to sell to real customer need and to do so without deception or product cramming. Don't promise more than you know we can deliver, and if the fit isn't good, don't make the sale. Go for win-win every time. We'll back you up."

The second message is a lot blunter: "Make the quota. We don't care how you do it. Just get the numbers."

Salespeople hear both these messages, but when it's three days to quota, guess which one they take seriously? Because their companies have made it clear that priority 1 is meeting the numbers, they take the "win-win" message for the lip service that it is, and they go out and make the sale at any cost. Two months later, when the customer screams that the dynamite service he or she was promised isn't coming through, or the problem that needed fixing has grown worse, senior management points a finger at the "deceptive" salesperson: "Look at the trouble *you've* gotten us into, once again."

It's not a very frank or open system, and like most systems that lack these qualities, it's not very productive either. Seeing sales professionals as client killers, sending them out into the "trenches" to do the dirty work, rewarding them with fat commissions but demeaning their labor—all of this generates an atmosphere of resentment and confusion that artificially divorces sales from the business proper and allows everyone—general and sales management included—to forget who provides the company with its basic fuel. The only reason that businesses have gotten away with this charade up to now is that they have enjoyed the benefits of relatively light competition and a customer base that didn't know any better.

As the old cowboy once put it, "Them days is closing fast." In the last twenty years alone, this traditional business approach has had to endure the onslaughts of a communications explosion, two oil crises, the death of the rust belt, the Tokyo *Blitzkrieg*, Ralph Nader, and the most dramatic technological revolution in history. Any company that thinks it can compete in this radically changed atmosphere by treating sales as merely a necessary evil should look for a Chapter 11 lawyer right away.

THE KEY TO THE FUTURE: PULLING TOGETHER

There is a better way to do things. The secret of that better way is *integration*. Not the "vertical" or "horizontal" integration that the economists talk about. The integration we mean is the pulling together of senior management not only with its own sales professionals but with the major clients those professionals are in touch with. What is needed is a team approach to revenue management, one which recognizes that excellence today is built on enduring *partnerships*, not the numbers game that has often been the norm.

You want your company to be alive in ten years? Here's a program to ensure that it will happen.

Step 1. Listen to the hunters.

Everything has to start with the revenue stream, and nobody knows more about your revenues than the people who interact with your major accounts. So it makes no sense to design "strategies" for key customers without listening to what your salespeople say about them. They're the only ones who can tell you what an account really needs, and they're the only ones who can tell you what decision makers in the account feel about your proposals and your company. As markets shrink and competition heats up, you can't afford to ignore this on-the-ground input. Without it, "close to the customer" is just a phrase.

Thanks to the disastrous experiences with quality control that beset American car manufacturers in the 1970s, the Big Three now regularly involve their assembly-line workers in the targeting and resolution of production problems; they've discovered that the people who make the cars actually know what works and what doesn't. It's time for a similar newsflash regarding selling.

You want to know what they think in Peoria? Ask someone who's been there. And then listen like you've never listened before.

Step 2. Take account management seriously.

You don't do that by creating twenty-pound account "plans" that are obsolete the minute they're written. Or by giving your best producer a paper promotion and calling her the Rydell account manager. You do it by institutionalizing team involvement in the analysis and targeting of major business. In account management that is worthy of the name, all the key figures who can impact on an account's revenue meet periodically to implement strategies for improving it. And they do so under the direction of an individual whose only job is to manage that account, not just for this quarter but for the duration.

We're stressing here what no one else has bothered to. We're calling for something far more radical, organizationally speaking, than a new nameplate or a slight expansion of responsibility. The "account manager" that we're describing isn't a salesperson of the year with a new hat. He or she is an upper-level management professional who works full time on the care and feeding of one customer. Who coordinates all activities that relate to that account, from sales and marketing to research, service, and troubleshooting. Who reports directly to *senior* management. *And* who is as valued and respected in the organization as any senior line or staff manager. We're talking about a whole new career track. *That's* what we mean by taking it seriously.

Step 3. Get the blue suits out on the line.

Several years ago, when Australia's national airline, Qantas, was debating where to order $500 million worth of new planes, Boeing's chief executive officer flew to Canberra to meet personally with Australian authorities—including the country's prime minister. When his counterpart at the competition was asked to do the same, he responded, "That's what I have salespeople for." Box score after this episode: Boeing $500 million, competition zero.

In an atmosphere where the prizes are this significant, you've got to use executive muscle to secure major accounts. *Not* doing this says to the customer, "You're not important enough." Hence the Boeing CEO wings it to Canberra. Hewlett-Packard corporate vice presidents make executive calls *every quarter* on major customers. Coca-Cola's chief operating officer, Don Keough, and all other Coke senior executives keep in constant touch with their salespeople; they are active members of major account teams. Take a tip from these winners: If sales revenue matters to your company, spend at least one day a month with the sales force.

This isn't cosmetics, and it isn't some cutesy sales version of management by walking around. We're talking about rethinking—and restructuring—American business, top to bottom. "Hunters" and "chiefs" eating lunch together. It may sound unusual, but if you think you can secure major account revenue today without such integration, it won't be long before you're *out* to lunch.

Step 4. Turn your customers into partners.

What we mean by this goes way beyond the currently fashionable idea that you should sell to customer need. Of course you should do that: In the end it's the only way to stay in business. But it's not enough. You've got to look out for your own needs as well. The goal should be win-win relationships, where the interests of both your firms are well served. And—a critical but often overlooked element—where your customer is made *aware* of your intention to create joint ventures, rather than contests, with his or her firm.

This means breaking another hoary axiom and *sharing* your strategy with the account that you're working on. We mean it literally. In the most effective account teams that we know, the seller and the client work together to create solutions that will make both of them more profitable. Coke does it with customer advisory boards. Apple does it with user groups. The terminology is different, but the goal is the same: Tell the buyers how you're trying to serve them, and let them tell you how to do it better.

We hear two objections all the time. First, "You *can't* let the customer know what you're doing." Why not? Because tradition says keep one step ahead of the victim. Good advice for a sniper, maybe, or a drummer who never sees the same town twice. In a world where critical major accounts, repeat business and long-term relationships hold the keys to survival, it's an invitation to be blindsided by savvier, more "user-friendly" competitors.

Second objection: "Our customers wouldn't cooperate. They wouldn't help us set strategy for their business." You don't think so? Try them. The myth is that customers won't open up. The reality is that they're dying to tell you their problems, if they believe you can contribute to a solution. The most progressive selling organizations in this country are making this reality a part of every strategy. If you want to survive into the next century, you'll do it too.

Step 5. If you can't do it right, don't do it.

Growing accounts means investing: time, people hours, company resources. All of that is limited. Therefore, you need to focus on those sales opportunities with the best chance of providing good returns, and give them whatever resources they need. Not "whatever the budget will allow," but whatever will *get the job done*. At the same time, you've got to pull back from "opportunities" where the payoff is one chance in a million.

Neither of these imperatives is characteristic of American business. Typically, we've stretched ourselves thin by throwing too few dollars at too many projects: by taking *any* sale, no matter how low yield; most of all, by failing to *focus on what we do best*. Not one manager in a hundred will readily free up extra resources for prime accounts—no matter how great their potential. Not one manager in a thousand will readily let a sale go—no matter how much grief it's likely to cause. Result? Valuable people chasing sucker bets—and being deflected, every day, from solid business.

In defining the markets you're best positioned to compete in, sticking to the knitting is fundamental. But you have to know what the knitting is. That means asking your salespeople again. Listening to what they tell you. And making choices.

Step 6. Grow your accounts, don't pick at them.

Doing business with an account for the long haul means nurturing the possibilities for future business, not just writing today's orders and hoping for the best. Sometimes it means forgoing a deal because writing it would not be in your customer's (or your own) long-term interest. American companies have traditionally rejected this long view; subscribing to the William F. Cody school of selling, they've gone out, guns blazing, to "knock off" business the way Buffalo Bill knocked off his namesake animals, yelling "Get it while you can" out of one side of their mouths and "Damn the future" out of the other. Trouble is, this approach *does* damn the future.

It doesn't have to be that way. Ask any of the Japanese auto companies, which squeaked by on paper-thin profit margins for a decade while they strengthened their position with American consumers. Ask New York Life, which cemented its relationship with a giant textile company by continuing to carry their coverage through a near bankruptcy—and realized millions in new policies when the client restructured. These companies prospered by observing the same principle: By growing your customer's business, you're also growing your own.

Step 7. Retool the quota system.

The current quota system has got to go. We're not talking about quotas themselves. In providing incentive for salespeople and in helping to forecast account revenues, quotas can be valuable management tools. But like many tools, they can also be turned into weapons; when they function less as incentives than as threats, their utility vanishes in a sea of numbers-chasing. Yes, you have to look at the quarterly numbers. But when the numbers are more important than anything else, you're in trouble.

In a sensible quota system, the numbers don't descend from above, like printouts from some great computer in the sky. Realistic quotas are set jointly by everyone concerned with account revenues. That means sales management, senior management, *and* the line salespeople who must meet them. Businesses that involve field people in the setting of their own quotas have found consistently that good salespeople *want* a stretch quota; they just don't want it imposed on them by pinheads in pinstripes.

In a sensible quota system, the numbers are the result of strategic thinking: They answer such questions as "Where do we want to be positioned with this account two years from now?" Not just "How much can we *get out of them* this quarter?" A strategically generated quota system gives you numbers that are tied to reality. A system that sets the numbers *before* the strategy creates "strategies" that are merely justifications for the numbers; it also makes it virtually impossible for the sales force to sell to real customer need.

In a sensible quota system, the reward mechanism is tied not just to individual performance but to the "growing" of an account relationship over time. Obviously this involves teamwork. We need fewer Caribbean trips for "sales-person of the year" and more for "account team of the year." The last thing American business needs is more hotshot free agents, jumping from company to company like superstar athletes jump from franchise to franchise in search of the latest eight-figure contract. That builds ego, not performance.

Finally, in a sensible quota system, it's *reality*, not "projections," that makes the difference. Reacting to that on-the-ground input that only field people can provide, account teams set quotas that are not only doable but that consider the *customer's* needs as well as the seller's. We need stretch, and aggressiveness, and market ingenuity, sure. We don't need any more numbers jockeys who say "I don't care if the grass is getting thin. You got us eight buffalo last month. Now get us nine."

Where does this leave us, in the end?

It leaves us, we immodestly suggest, with a choice. One option is to continue down the well-worn path of tradition. On that path, major accounts are handled piecemeal and haphazardly. Business strategy and sales strategy are distant cousins. So-called account managers are rewarded for making the numbers, not for long-term management. And sales professionals, who are the only people in any business who really know the customer, are seen as slick and not quite reputable corporate cat's-paws.

The attractiveness of this option is that it seems cheap: You don't have to make any changes at all to put it into place. It's already there, nudging many companies toward obsolescence.

The other option is to remake the corporation. No point in pulling punches. The seven-step program we have outlined means totally reassessing managerial responsibilities as they impact on the generation of account revenue. It means recognizing that those revenues—every company's lifeblood—must be managed by full-time, senior-level professionals. It means jettisoning the ancient bias against the salesperson, redefining that critical player's role so that he or she can deliver for your company *and* the customer instead of playing the heavy in some number-juggler's pipe dream.

It means recognizing, above all, that business works when the real needs of real people are being satisfied. It means taking "close to the customer" not as a slogan but as a practical, urgent imperative—a key to account success for the duration.

The money is there, and so are the resources. The question is culture. With so many decades, so much habit and hypocrisy, and so many careers invested in keeping sales out of the loop, can we ever learn to pull together, to grow the future?

The real question is: Can we afford *not* to?

Index

For further information on LAMP, please contact:

Miller Heiman, Inc.,
1595 Meadow Wood Lane, Suite 2
Reno, NV 89502
1-800-526-6400